From Millennial to Millionaire: DIY 401(k)

From Millennial to Millionaire: DIY 401(k)

**FIVE DO-IT-YOURSELF STEPS FOR THE DIGITAL
GENERATION TO DESIGN AND MANAGE THEIR 401(K)**

Matthew K. Miller

ISBN-13: 9780692912133
ISBN-10: 0692912134
Library of Congress Control Number: 2017910269
DIY Millionaire, LLC, Chicago, IL
Printed in the United States of America.
First Printing: 2017
DIY Millionaire, LLC
https://www.thediymillionaire.com

Disclaimer

This book is not intended to be a substitute for personalized advice from a professional financial planner. Nothing contained within this text should be construed as financial advice. The publisher and author make no representation or warranty as to this book's adequacy or appropriateness for any purpose. Similarly, no representation or warranty is made as to the accuracy of the material in this book.

Purchasing this book does not create a client relationship or other advisory, fiduciary, or professional services relationship with the publisher or the author. *You alone* bear *sole* responsibility of assessing the merits and risks associated with any financial decisions you make. And you should always keep in mind that any investment can result in partial or complete loss.

Dedication

To Joe Miller (1949–2012), my beloved father.

Contents

Disclaimer · **v**

Dedication · **vii**

Figures · **xv**

Preface and Acknowledgments · **xvii**

Introduction From Millennial to Millionaire · **1**

Step 1 Yes, *you* can DIY your 401(k) · **9**

You own your retirement · **9**

What's a 401(k)? · 10

A portrait of two millennial investors · · · · · · · · · · · · · · · 12

Further details about your 401(k) · 13

What it takes to be a DIY investor · **20**

Values matter the most · 22

Build your DIY investing knowledge...for free! · · · · · · · · 22

Act now and adjust later · 24

Summary · **25**

Step 2 How much to save for retirement · · · · · · · · · · · · · · · · · **27**

What kind of retirement do you want? · · · · · · · · · · · · · · · · · **27**

Start to save for retirement now! · **29**

Contribute at least your employer's match · · · · · · · · · · · · 30

How to pay off student debt and save for retirement · · · · 32

Tips to help you achieve a 10–15 percent savings rate · · · 33

Why saving 10–15 percent of your annual salary is crucial · · · · **34**

How to budget like a millionaire to put this all into practice · · **36**

Example millennial budget · 38

Interpreting the budget · 38

Caution: What you see in the future isn't what you always get · **40**

Compounding accelerates earnings growth · · · · · · · · · · · 40

Inflation brings earnings down · · · · · · · · · · · · · · · · · · · 42

Summary · **44**

Step 3 Choose the right 401(k) account option · · · · · · · · · · · · · · **46**

The two flavors of the 401(k) you need to know · · · · · · · · · **46**

Choose either a traditional or a Roth 401(k) · · · · · · · · · · · · **49**

A traditional is good for late savers and tax
savings today · 52

A Roth is best for early investors and tax benefits in
retirement · 53

Still can't decide? Read this! · **54**

When should you do a Roth in-plan conversion? · · · · · · · · · · **55**

**Nonprofit and government-employee options: 403(b),
457, TSP** · **56**

Summary · **57**

Step 4 Design your 401(k) for millionaire success · · · · · · · · · · · · · · · **59**

Enroll in your 401(k) ASAP · **59**

Be an "aggressive investor" to accumulate millions · · · · · · · · **61**

Three ingredients to build your investment portfolio · · · · · · · **64**

Allocate your assets toward stock · · · · · · · · · · · · · · · · · · · 65

Diversify your allocation among domestic and inter-
national stock · 67

Select the low-cost investments your plan offers · · · · · · · · 68

What fees do you pay in your 401(k)? · · · · · · · · · · · · · · · · · · · **70**

401(k) fees· 71

How can you lower your 401(k) costs?· · · · · · · · · · · · · · · 72

The Fiduciary Rule in one paragraph · · · · · · · · · · · · · · · 72

How to design your millionaire 401(k) portfolio today · · · · · · **73**

The Target-Date Retirement Fund Portfolio · · · · · · · · · · 73

The Index Funds-Only Portfolio · · · · · · · · · · · · · · · · · 74

The Hybrid Index Funds and Lowest-Cost Actively
Managed Funds Portfolio · 74

Investments to avoid in your twenties and thirties · · · · · · 75

Three tips to boost your returns · · · · · · · · · · · · · · · · · · · **76**

Mid-cap mutual funds are the "sweet spot" · · · · · · · · · · · 76

Take advantage of the "small-cap premium" · · · · · · · · · · 77

Select to reinvest your company stock dividends · · · · · · · 77

Summary · **78**

Step 5 Manage your 401(k) for continued success · · · · · · · · · · · · · · **80**

Rebalance to keep your portfolio fit · · · · · · · · · · · · · · · · · **80**

Digital options for managing your wealth · · · · · · · · · · · · · · **82**

Avoid these common 401(k) mistakes! · · · · · · · · · · · · · · · · **83**

When to do a 401(k) rollover · **84**

Congratulate yourself on your success · · · · · · · · · · · · · · · · · · 86

Summary · 86

FAQs on addressing millennials' concerns · · · · · · · · · · · · · · · · 89

Quick start guide to begin your 401(k) investing ASAP! · · · · · 91

Certificate of Completion for DIY 401(k)· · · · · · · · · · · · · · · · 95

DIY 401(k) Math · 97

Case 1: You'll be a millionaire if you start investing
at age twenty-two · 97

Case 2: You might not be a millionaire if you wait
until age thirty-five · 98

Case 3: But you can catch up at age thirty-five!
However, you'll have to save a lot more · · · · · · · · · · · · · · · 98

Case 4: You lose free money by not contributing up
to your employer's match· 99

Case 5: You can maximize your 401(k) growth by
contributing 10–15 percent · 100

Case 6: Inflation brings your 401(k) earnings down· · · · · 101

Case 7: Consider why a traditional 401(k) might
work best · 102

Case 8: Or, see why maybe a Roth works better for you · 103

Case 9: Be an aggressive investor while you are young· · · 104

Glossary · 107

Recommended Resources · 113

    Retirement guides· 113

    Digital wealth-management platforms· · · · · · · · · · · · · · · 113

    Financial blogs· 114

    Data sources · 114

About the Author· 115

Endnotes · 117

Figures

Figure 1:   Pension versus 401(k) comparison · · · · · · · · · · · · · · · ·21

Figure 2:   Cost of waiting to invest until age thirty-five · · · · · · · · · · ·24

Figure 3:   Relationship between contribution rate and future
401(k) balance ·35

Figure 4:   Stock market return chart (1950–2016) · · · · · · · · · · · · · ·40

Figure 5:   Compounding of $1,000 over forty-five years at 8
percent investment return ·41

Figure 6:   Inflation rate chart (1950–2016) · · · · · · · · · · · · · · · · · · ·43

Figure 7:   Relationship between contribution rate and real
401(k) balance ·43

Figure 8:   Traditional versus Roth 401(k) effect on take-home pay · ·48

Figure 9:   Traditional 401(k) versus Roth 401(k) comparison · · · · ·51

Figure 10: 401(k) balance in 100 percent stocks versus 100
percent bonds over ten to fifty years · · · · · · · · · · · · · · · ·66

Preface and Acknowledgments

I began to write this book in the summer of 2016 to combine my two passions: investing and writing. My education is in economics and business; I work in the financial services industry, and I moonlight as a writer. I was quickly enthralled with personal finance in college, and so I have been a do-it-yourself (DIY) investor since I entered the professional workforce in 2010. Since then, I've learned that investing requires no more than five simple steps to grow my wealth over time to ensure that I retire as a millionaire. This book was born to inform and inspire you to become a DIY investor too.

Investing, along with personal finance in general, is a broad and rich topic, but many books give only marginal attention to certain facets of it—for example, the intricacies of 401(k) investing. To address this gap, I focus exclusively here on investing for retirement through the 401(k) account. I have had much success in this area, and since my first job out of college, I have contributed to my 401(k) and learned about its technical nuances and its pleasing wealth-building qualities. With it, I have laid the foundation for a secure and comfortable retirement. And you can too, and with that acknowledged, I want to first and foremost thank you, the reader, for joining in on my personal DIY investing experience and story and for taking the first step on yours, as well. You'll see that DIY 401(k) investing is understandable, easy, and even enjoyable!

I am grateful to the many friends and family who have read and reviewed this book. Much appreciation goes out to Rachel Miller, Matti Shicker, and Alexandra Ross for their dedicated review and feedback.

Added thanks to Michael Zuckerman for reviewing the book twice, providing substantive feedback and needed copyedits. And I am incredibly appreciative to Elyse Krug Miller for her multiple rounds of reading and editing and for her probing insights on how to make this book more compelling.

I have attempted to make this book, first, accessible to the millennial generation, and, second, thorough enough so that you will understand my recommendations as well as the reasoning behind them. It is my hope that you will acquire the DIY mentality and capabilities to feel confident and competent to take your 401(k) investing into your own hands going forward. Each reviewer has contributed substantially to these goals!

Additional heartfelt thanks to my technical editor, Michael Oxman, whose encouraging feedback has been invaluable to this book's development. Michael's keen perspective offered insightful, critical thought that helped to shape this book's content and format. Our fruitful conversations helped to refine its focus, recommendations, and technical integrity. Any and all blunders are my own, of course.

I want to give a shout out to my social media consultant, Danielle Perlin-Good. She has helped to elevate my social media skills, and provided needed strategic advice and personal coaching on how to build the best digital presence for this book. For more information on her digital marketing consulting and freelance writing, you can visit https://www.danielleperlin.com.

I am forever grateful to my late father, to whom this book is dedicated. In the last ten years of his life, he learned on his own the very important financial advice embedded in this book, exemplifying that it takes personal accountability and a bit of initiative to cultivate and self-manage your money and investing for long-term success. He was the least materialistic person I have known, but he always told me "not to worship money but to understand its importance." I live by that example today. Thank you, Dad, for your wisdom, and may your memory be a blessing.

INTRODUCTION

From Millennial to Millionaire

*F*rom Millennial to Millionaire: DIY 401(k) is focused more than anything else on do-it-yourself (DIY) investing for millennials. Millennials need to invest to achieve their retirement goals. As a generation, these are young adults born between 1979 and 2000,[1] and many are keen to understand what retirement planning and investing is all about to take ownership over their financial lives. They want the knowledge and capability that go along with the mentality for self-directing their investing to fit their personal needs.

In this book, I address the unique financial concerns of this generation, such as getting started now and continuously improving with investing, paying down student debt while saving for retirement, and getting disciplined with budgeting, among other anxieties. But I focus very specifically on a crucial investment account that you should become well acquainted with: the employer-sponsored 401(k). This is because the 401(k) is most likely your first exposure to investment accounts and to investing in general. And so it is key that you master the 401(k)'s intricacies to use it to its highest wealth-building potential. I will take you through five simple do-it-yourself steps that do just that.

If you work for an employer that offers you a 403(b), 457, or TSP account instead of the 401(k), the five steps still apply to you similarly. I'll cover the slight variations between the retirement accounts in Step 3 at a high level, so keep reading!

Why should you read this book in the first place? At this point in your life, perhaps you've graduated from college and started your first job. Maybe you've been even more adventurous, and gotten married,

1

bought a house, and started a family. But you may not have paid quite enough attention to your 401(k). If not, that is worrisome. If I can't stress anything more, it is that the 401(k) is the most substantial road to your retirement security, especially if you're a millennial. Employers have overwhelmingly abandoned pensions, which used to provide defined retirement income for employees. My book is your comprehensive and actionable guide to getting your 401(k) started, funded, and managed. By picking up this book, you're further ahead than most!

While the notion of retirement is changing, meaning that research from the Transamerica Center for Retirement Studies shows that millennials will opt not to withdraw from the workforce entirely in an ever increasing knowledge economy but continue to work in some smaller capacity,[2] the income that you will rely on to sustain you will most certainly come from the earnings of your 401(k) account. (If you don't rely on this vehicle, then you may be living solely off meager benefits from Social Security, whose future is uncertain.) So it is essential that you learn how to properly save enough and invest smartly in your 401(k) to prepare for a comfortable and assured retirement.

Where do millennials stand in terms of understanding and using their 401(k)s as a means to achieve their retirement goals? Statistics about this generation's retirement readiness are both promising and troublesome. On the positive side, millennials are demonstrating the sensible behaviors of emerging super savers. Further research from the Transamerica Center for Retirement Studies shows that they are getting an impressive jump start on their 401(k) retirement planning and investing. Here are some indicators:

1. Fifty-four percent report retirement saving as their top financial priority, higher than covering basic living expenses (52 percent) or even paying off student loans (20 percent).[3]
2. Sixty-eight percent are "very" or "somewhat" confident that they will be able to fully retire someday with a comfortable lifestyle.[4]
3. Seventy-two percent participate in an employer-sponsored 401(k) if offered one.[5]
4. Twenty-two is the median age that millennials start to save for retirement.[6]

So millennials should take pride in what is clearly an already commendable state of affairs. Naysayers may call millennials completely unprepared for retirement, but we observe from the research that they are confident about their readiness. We've seen that they prioritize retirement savings and start to save in their early twenties. However, the research also reveals opportunities for improvement through more insight and education:

1. Millennials save 7 percent of their annual salaries in 401(k)s, but that may not be enough savings to cover retirement needs.[7]
2. Sixty percent use some form of professional management service, leading to higher account expenses and lower investment returns.[8]
3. Twenty-two percent have taken loans or early withdrawals from 401(k)s, impeding long-term 401(k) growth and compounding.[9]
4. Twenty-five percent are "unsure" how their retirement investments are allocated, and 22 percent invest mostly in bonds and other stable investments, which is an improper asset allocation for long-term growth.[10]
5. The median amount that millennials believe they need for retirement is $500,000, which is not enough to sustain them for a projected twenty to thirty years.[11]

In these two data sets, we see a contradiction: millennials expect to need only $500,000 at retirement, yet they start investing in 401(k)s early—at age twenty-two. As you will learn in this book, the dissonance between these data points suggests that millennials (1) don't know how much they really need to save and (2) don't understand that starting to invest at age twenty-two can result in a portfolio value way above $500,000. These two data points are at odds with one another because, in fact, someone investing that early can be well on his or her way to retiring as a millionaire. How so?

To answer that question, my book provides research-based objective information, supplemented by my own commentary on my philosophy and personal experience with investing, and hopefully, compelling storytelling along the way that encourages and motivates you to get started.

But if there were three takeaways about retirement planning and investing that you should take to heart from this book, they would be as follows:

1. **Invest early and consistently.** Start to invest in your 401(k) as early as possible in your career, and invest consistently over time with automatic salary deferrals. The more time you have to invest, the more of the awesome power of compounding you get.

2. **Invest at least 10–15 percent of your salary every year.** Investing anything is better than nothing at all, but as we will see in detail in Step 2, I will show you why investing 10–15 percent of your pay is so crucial. I'll even provide tips on how to incrementally get there over time.

3. **Invest for the long term, and stay calm.** To get the highest return for your 401(k) investments, you'll need to take some calculated risk and invest almost exclusively in the stock market while you're in your twenties and thirties. Even with short-term fluctuations, the long-term stock market return has been 8 percent. Of course, past performance doesn't guarantee future returns, but still, stay the course calmly when the market gets turbulent in the short term.

With these three takeaways alone, you can go from a millennial to a millionaire by the time you retire. And in this book, I will help you get there so you can follow the positive millennial behavior trends and avoid the pitfalls. Here's what you'll learn:

-   **Step 1** shows you how to build your DIY mentality and how to get started investing in your 401(k) account.
-   **Step 2** helps you define your retirement-income needs and provides guidance on how much to save and budget.
-   **Step 3** demonstrates how to determine what type of 401(k) account is best for your specific financial and tax situation.
-   **Step 4** provides direction on how to design a diversified 401(k) portfolio that maximizes returns and lowers costs.
-   **Step 5** demonstrates how you can self-manage your account so that your portfolio value stays aligned to your personalized goals.

Additionally, I provide bonus features such as the following:

- Summaries and key takeaways for each step that paraphrase the key points you need to get started on DIY 401(k) investing
- A FAQ list to address millennials' concerns about 401(k) investing
- A quick start guide that distills all this book's information into a one-stop shop checklist to get you started ASAP
- An appendix that goes through all the mathematics so that you too can easily replicate what is in this book in Microsoft Excel
- Recommended resources and a glossary to help you expand your investing self-education from here

After reading this book, you will know how to generate wealth and retirement income on your own. You won't need to lean on your parents for any financing once you graduate from college. You won't need expensive professional services to manage your 401(k). And you won't fall for the risky behaviors that I see all too often today, such as short-term day trading, complex options speculation, and strategies that try to time the market. Instead, you will be self-sufficient, with the competence and confidence to do it yourself as a millennial investor who prizes sensible long-term investing strategies.[12]

Here's another bonus: when you complete *From Millennial to Millionaire: DIY 401(k)* and possess the knowledge to implement the five steps to become a successful DIY investor to design and manage your 401(k), you'll find a certificate of completion to trigger you to start now. Once you've read the entire book, sign and date your certificate.

Know that you are not alone. With the growth of independent financial media, the popularity of tax-advantaged retirement accounts, and the surge of free wealth-management platforms, the journey to significant wealth has never been more democratic. It's even more accelerated by low barriers to entry, free access to open-source knowledge, and the digital resources available today. Growing wealth is easy because long-term investment advice is so readily and freely available online. It is simple because long-term investing rests on a set of simple principles. And it is seamless because digital-technology experiences power and support all personal finance today.[13]

This book will be of especially excellent service to the following readers:

- Recent college graduates in their early to midtwenties who are eager to learn DIY investing, understand their 401(k) plan, and start their journey toward financial empowerment
- Young professionals in their late twenties and even late thirties who need to catch up or want a new perspective on their 401(k) investing
- Workers who currently aren't offered a 401(k) but, when and if offered one, want to be as knowledgeable as possible to get started ASAP

However, although it is still useful, this book does not provide answers or recommendations for those who are in more complex financial situations. These may include married couples seeking joint retirement planning advice, millennials who inherit retirement accounts from deceased relatives, or entrepreneurs in need of retirement account options, to name a few. These situations may require the use of a professional tax or financial advisor. Furthermore, this book does not cover brokerage account options, known as "brokerage windows," that may be available in any given 401(k) plan, because that material gets into more advanced territory not suited for a beginner DIY investor.

Any section in this book where I recommend you work with a tax or financial advisor is marked as **Get Professional Assistance.** Regarding a 401(k) plan, there are various situations in this book in which I recommend you get professional assistance:

- A 401(k) withdrawal (see Step 1)
- A Roth in-plan conversion (see Step 3)
- A 401(k) rollover (see Step 5)

Beyond those situations, millennials today, more so than ever before, are in an excellent position to take advantage of DIY 401(k) investing. It is my hope that the financial literacy you will gain here will serve you for many years to come.

With that said, let's get started on your journey to financial empow-erment! And, for more DIY personal finance information and detailed reading to supplement your *DIY 401(k)*, feel free to check out my blog at https://www.thediymillionaire.com. For more real-time engagement you can find me on Twitter @MatthewKMiller. Enjoy!

STEP 1

Yes, *you* can DIY your 401(k)

You own your retirement

In today's world, *you* are responsible for your own retirement readiness and security. This sense of obligation may seem unnerving, but it doesn't need to be daunting. In fact, the more truthfully you acknowledge that you are the driver of your financial future, and gradually internalize the responsibilities that accompany self-directed retirement planning and investing, the better off you will be to provide for and sustain yourself in the far-off future. And you might not have thought it possible, but yes, *you* can DIY your 401(k).

The overwhelming majority of 401(k) plans are self-directed, which means that you are in control of the amount that's contributed to the account, how that contribution is invested, and the management of the account to ensure the account is optimally performing over time to reach your retirement goals. Given that you have this personal autonomy to steer your 401(k) and that the account is self-directed in nature, there's an even greater case to become as highly proficient of a DIY investor as you possibly can.

My goal is to help empower, inspire, and coach you in Step 1 to build the basic knowledge, mentality, and skills to grow and develop into your DIY investor persona. The first discussion that we need to have to start this conversation on DIY investing, even before we anatomize the 401(k), is to understand the basic definitions between investing and investment accounts, because these two concepts provide a frame of reference for what a 401(k) is. And then secondly, we will dig deeper into the details of how a 401(k) is constructed and how it operates. We will finalize the conversation with the three ingredients you need to begin to cultivate and mature your DIY investing finesse.

Investing

Investing is defined as deferring your pay today to save for the future, with the expectation that you will get more money back in return. But it's not just ordinary saving like opening a checking or savings account at your local bank, which may provide you with a 1 percent or less return. When you invest, you are instead putting your money in the stock market. When you strategize for retirement, you must lean on investing to achieve long-term results. Saving alone will not help you achieve your retirement goals.

Investment Account

An investment account is a type of financial account where you invest, with the goal to achieve long-term capital accumulation. There are many types of investment accounts, and in this book, we will focus on the 401(k) account, which you will use for your retirement planning and investing. An investment account provides investment funds, like stocks, bonds, and mutual funds, and holds your investment assets over time.

What's a 401(k)?

A 401(k) is an employer-sponsored retirement plan. It's a great way to start your DIY investing journey, as well as an attractive investment account. Let's look at four key points that make the 401(k) the go-to retirement plan for many American workers, especially for millennials. Knowing this will help you to build your DIY competencies.[14]

A 401(k) Is an Employer-Sponsored Retirement Plan.

Your employer sponsors a 401(k) as a benefit of employment that is meant to help its employees invest for retirement. In the private sector, the 401(k) has become the mainstream retirement plan, replacing the traditional pension plan. With a 401(k), the responsibility is on you to enroll, contribute, and invest in your plan. Your employer may make you wait for a certain period (for example, at least a year) before you can start contributing, or it may let you start contributing right after your hire date. You will want to understand from your employer when you are eligible to enroll in your 401(k) plan.

A 401(k) Is a Tax-Favored Investment Account.

You'll pay taxes on the money in your 401(k), but the account is "tax advantaged." There are two 401(k) account options: the traditional and the Roth. In the traditional, your contributions (i.e., what you put into your account) are pretax, but you pay ordinary income tax on the withdrawals (i.e., what you take out of your account at retirement). However, in the Roth, your contributions are after-tax, but your withdrawals are tax-free. This allows your investment earnings to grow tax deferred in the traditional and tax-free in the Roth. When you contribute to your 401(k) plan, you get to benefit from this rare favorable tax treatment by the Internal Revenue Service (IRS).

A 401(k) Is a Long-Term Saving Commitment.

A 401(k) is more than just an investment account. It is also a thirty-to-forty-year commitment to the prosperity of your future finances. Think of it as a container for you to invest your money in over time. Your plan will offer a menu of preselected investments; these will primarily be mutual funds (i.e., collections of stocks or bonds) that you can choose to build your investment portfolio based on your retirement goals, age, and risk tolerance. A 401(k) account is not a checking account or a savings account that you can easily withdraw money out of. Keep your money in your 401(k) for the long-term.

A 401(k) Is a Great Way to Build Wealth into the Millions.

You can accumulate significant wealth through your 401(k). First, your employer may provide a matching contribution, which is free money to you. (Not all employers do this, and if they do, how much they match is at their discretion.) Second, if you start your investing early, you have the advantage of the power of compounding over long periods. Compounding is when money makes money on itself. Third, your 401(k) contributions come directly out of your salary through salary deferrals so that you can invest consistently each pay period. With that, you get the added benefit of dollar-cost averaging, which lowers the average cost that you pay for your investments over time.

A portrait of two millennial investors

To demonstrate the point that you can build significant wealth through your 401(k), let's follow the stories of Eve and Adam, two fictitious millennial investors. I'll lean on these two characters throughout the book to help illustrate the decisions that you will make to design and manage your 401(k). Here, we have two different millennial investors whom we meet often: one who is prudent, and another who is a procrastinator.

Here's Eve: Eve started her career right after college with a Fortune 500 company and enrolled in her 401(k) immediately. She has contributed 7 percent of every paycheck, and her employer contributes by matching 100 percent of the first 4 percent of eligible pay. Assuming her salary averages $47,000 per year across her whole career, between the ages of twenty-two and sixty-seven, her 401(k) balance grows to $2,287,499.42 by the time she retires. Voilà! She has far more than $500,000. In fact, she is a DIY 401(k) millionaire.[15]

But then, there's Adam: He joined Eve's company, too, with the same average lifetime salary ($47,000) and the same level of matching contributions from the firm. But Adam waited until age thirty-five to start investing in his 401(k), and he contributed only 6 percent annually. Yes, he saved enough to meet the employer's matching contribution (4 percent) plus a bit more, but he's below the millennial median (7 percent). By age sixty-seven, even with thirty-two years of investing, his 401(k) balance is worth only $698,248.11.[16] If he wants to catch up to Eve, he can, even though he started a lot later, but he would have to save considerably more than she does per year—29 percent of the same annual salary—to do that.[17]

What's the secret sauce that catapulted Eve's 401(k) balance to an exceptionally higher value than Adam's? Well, it's time and a concept known as compounding. When you are young, you have time on your side to let your investments grow to their highest potential. A thirteen-year delay in investing in his 401(k) cost Adam more than a million dollars—$1,589,251.31 (= $2,287,499.42 – $698,248.11)! It's your choice, who do you want to be? Eve or Adam? I hope after reading this book you choose Eve.

To keep the exposition and analysis in this book as closely aligned to the reality of the average millennial investor, all the examples throughout this book where we will encounter Eve and Adam will rely on the following technical assumptions:

- Median millennial salary is $47,000.[18]
- Employer's matching contribution is 100 percent on 4 percent of eligible pay.[19]
- Retirement age is sixty-seven.[20]
- Stock market investment return is 8 percent.[21]

These numbers are used only for illustrative purposes. Your personal statistics might be different. Check out DIY 401(k) Math at the end of this book where I expand on the mathematics presented here with case studies. The case studies will follow Eve and Adam. You can calibrate the Excel formulas there to fit your own personalized financial situation (i.e., salary, contribution rate, employer's match, current age, and expected retirement age).

Further details about your 401(k)

With those key points in mind, let's continue with a more detailed examination of your 401(k). To design and manage your 401(k) plan better, you need to know it. By now, you should know that a 401(k) account is a type of salary-deferral plan set up by a private-sector employer to help you, the employee, save for retirement and that these plans are generally self-directed. Additionally, you know that the

401(k) plan offers tax advantages not often provided by the IRS to incentivize you to save.[22]

In the next discussion, let's review in detail the 401(k)'s structure, plan sponsorship and administration, plan provider, annual contribution limits, participation eligibility, vesting schedules, investment options, withdrawal rules, and more. Keep in mind that the IRS has the discretion to change these rules each year.[23]

The 401(k) Plan Sponsor

The plan sponsor is generally your employer that offers a 401(k) plan. The plan sponsor will determine eligibility requirements, what percentage of your salary you can contribute, whether to match contributions and at how much of eligible pay, whether to offer a Roth 401(k), when plan participants are vested and the investment funds provided in the plan, among other plan features. The plan sponsor generally acts as the plan administrator, too, and they need to ensure that the plan complies with the provisions of the Employee Retirement Income Security Act (ERISA), the federal law that governs qualified retirement plans.[24] Your plan sponsor will also choose the plan provider to partner with to offer the plan.[25]

The 401(k) Plan Provider

Your plan sponsor will partner with a 401(k) plan provider, usually a financial services company (i.e., Fidelity, Morgan Stanley, Wells Fargo, etc.) to operate day-to-day administration, enrollment, account servicing, and recordkeeping services. The plan provider holds plan participants' assets. Since plans are generally self-directed, it will be on the plan provider's website where plan participants choose their contribution percentage, research and select investment funds, and monitor 401(k) performance.[26]

The 401(k) Plan Advisor

Your 401(k) plan may also select to hire a plan advisor in addition to the plan provider. The plan advisor may help conduct 401(k) enrollments, encourage employees to participate in the plan, and advise on invest-ment fund selection. Or you may have access to a team of investment professionals, provided by the plan provider, that do roughly the same thing—manage and adjust your investments.[27]

Who Can Participate in a 401(k) Plan

If an employer offers a 401(k) plan, federal law requires that it provide equal employee access to enrollment and investing. However, the employer may impose two restrictions: participants may be required to have at least a full year of employment there (around a thousand hours over twelve months) and be at least twenty-one years old before they are allowed to contribute to that company's 401(k). Find out when you can opt in.[28]

Your Annual Contributions

There are annual contribution limits to what you can contribute to your 401(k).[29] For example, in 2017, if you are under fifty years old, you can contribute up to $18,000 per year. Of course, you are not required to contribute the maximum annual contribution. (For reference only, if you are fifty or older, you can add on a "catch-up" contribution of $6,000, for a total of up to $24,000 per year.) The IRS adjusts annual contribu-tion limits according to changes in inflation. Make sure to check the maximum limits every year.

Employer's Matching Contributions

When you contribute to the plan, your employer may provide a match-ing contribution. Employers are not required to provide a matching con-tribution on the employee's behalf. But if offered, then your employer decides how much to match. For example, they may match 100 percent of the first 4 percent of eligible pay, but each plan's matching schedule is unique. Additionally, your employer may offer nonelective contribu-tions. You will receive this contribution regardless of whether you con-tribute to the plan or not. To illustrate, let's say your employer makes a 3 percent nonelective contribution on your behalf even if you don't elect to contribute to your 401(k).

What Percentage of Your Take-Home Pay You Can Contribute

The plan sponsor decides how much of your pay you can contribute to your 401(k) plan each pay period. Usually, that cap is 10 percent or 15 percent of your gross pay, although it varies from plan to plan. For example, you may be allowed to contribute up to 50 percent of your take-home salary each pay period (up until you've met the legal annual contribution limits). So your employee contribution is limited to the lower of (1) the maximum percentage your employer permits each year, or (2) the dollar amount of the annual contribution limit. For example, if you make $47,000 per year and your employer allows you to contribute up to 15 percent of your salary, your maximum employee contribution limit is $7,050, and not the annual limit of $18,000 in 2017.

Types of Investments in a 401(k) Account

The plan sponsor is legally required to select the plan's investment funds. The most common type of fund offered is a mutual fund. Most plans offer at least three investment funds, while the average plan offers eight to twelve options. Most often you may see a mix of actively managed mutual funds, index mutual funds, target-date retirement funds, and the employing company's own stock (see Step 4). Additional investments that may be offered are stable value funds, guaranteed investment contracts (GICs), and variable annuities.[30]

How Your 401(k) Account Balance Grows

Your balance grows through your own contributions, your employer's matching contributions (if offered), and earnings from stock market gains and reinvested dividends. (The mutual funds in your plan always reinvest their gains or dividends, but if your account holds your company's stock, you have the option to elect to reinvest them.) As time goes on, your account will grow through a process called "compounding"—your earnings (market gains and losses) build on the account balance (earnings plus contributions).

What "Vesting" Means

We've just seen that your 401(k) balance is made up of three components:

1. Your employee contributions
2. Your employer's matching contributions (if offered)
3. Earnings from stock market gains and reinvested dividends

You are always entitled to your employee contributions and earnings should you ever decide to leave your employer. But you may not be entitled to keep your employer's matching contributions (and its earnings) until you are "vested." Your plan sponsor will determine when you are vested.

There are three flavors of vesting schedules you need to know:

- **Immediate.** You get to keep whatever money your employer matches immediately. For example, if you leave this job after six months, you are entitled to take the employer's match with you.[31]
- **Cliff.** You must wait for a particular moment before you get to take the employer's match with you if you leave. For example, you may have to work at your company for two years before you are vested at all, but at that point, you become 100 percent vested. In this case, if you leave before the two years, then you get none of your employer's match. If your employer offers a match under this rule, it must vest you within three years.[32]
- **Graded.** You get vested incrementally over time. For example, you may keep 20 percent of your employer's contributions (and its earnings) after two years, 40 percent after three years, and so forth. Vesting must occur over two to six years.[33]

401(k) Loans

A loan allows you to borrow money from your plan and repay it over time, generally within five years (unless you're using the money for a down payment on a house). A loan is not subject to ordinary income taxes or penalties, unless you do not repay the loan. You will pay interest on the loan amount back into your account. Setup and maintenance fees may also apply. You may take out up to half of an account's balance up to a maximum of $50,000. You pay back the loan through automatic deductions from your salary. But there are two caveats: (1), if you don't make a payment within a specific period of time, then the loan is considered a withdrawal and you may be subject to a 10 percent tax penalty and any applicable ordinary income taxes on the withdrawal, and (2), if you become separated from your job while the loan is outstanding, you must repay the entire thing within a specific period of time or incur the same penalty.

When You Can Withdraw Money from Your 401(k)

You can start, but are not required, to withdraw distributions from your 401(k) plan at age fifty-nine and a half without any tax penalty. These withdrawals are called "qualified distributions." You will pay any applicable ordinary income taxes on the withdrawal, if the account is a traditional. Of note, you will pay ordinary income taxes on the employer's match money from a Roth too.

Early Withdrawal Penalties

Your 401(k) may offer partial withdrawals. A partial withdrawal allows you to take out a proportion of your account balance; however, early withdrawals from both a traditional and Roth before age fifty-nine and a half may be subject to a 10 percent tax penalty. Additionally, for the traditional 401(k), early withdrawals will be subject to ordinary income taxes on both contributions and earnings; and for the Roth 401(k), early withdrawals will be subject to ordinary income taxes only on earnings. There is also the "age 55 rule," which states that if you retire or lose your job, at age fifty-five, you avoid the 10 percent early-withdrawal penalty. However, this applies only to your last employer's 401(k) and not to any other 401(k) in an earlier employer's plan.[34]

Hardship Withdrawals

A 401(k) plan may, but is not required to, additionally provide for hardship withdrawals. A hardship withdrawal is due to an immediate and significant financial need. Typically, all other loans and partial withdrawals must be taken out before a hardship withdrawal is allowed. If allowed, you may take hardship withdrawals, without the 10 percent tax penalty, if you meet one of the most common reasons:

1. You become permanently disabled.
2. You die (the distribution is sent to your estate or designated beneficiary).
3. Certain distributions sent to qualified military reservists called to active duty.
4. You have unreimbursed medical expenses that are more than 10 percent of your adjusted gross income, if under age sixty-five.[35]

Despite this provision, your 401(k) is the last account you want to take money from. You lose out on its tax-advantaged growth and compounding (see my blog article on how I saved $12,000 of emergency funds in 2016 to avoid withdrawing from my 401(k)).[36]

Get professional assistance: In this situation, I recommend that you consult with a tax or financial advisor prior to initiating a 401(k) partial or hardship withdrawal. Not all hardship withdrawals are exempt from the 10 percent tax penalty.

When You Must Withdraw From a 401(k)

While you can begin to take withdrawals from your 401(k) at age fifty-nine and a half, you don't have to. You can wait as long as until April 1 of the year after (1) the calendar year you reach age seventy and a half or (2) the calendar year in which you retire, whichever comes later. However, your plan may require you to receive distributions by age seventy and a half even if you have not retired. At that point, you must take out required minimum distributions (RMDs). This requirement applies to both the traditional and the Roth. You can withdraw more than the RMDs, though, but no less. The RMD is calculated based on your life expectancy.

What it takes to be a DIY investor

In your grandparents' generation (and perhaps your parents'), employers paid lifelong salaries to their employees after they retired. It was as if they had never left—except they didn't have to work anymore. This was done through a retirement account called a pension, which was a defined-benefit plan. The employer made contributions to it on an employee's behalf and essentially guaranteed a continuous flow of retirement payments, aka "benefits," for the remainder of his or her life. Sounds nice and cushy, no?

But those days are gone now. Ever since Congress enacted the 401(k) into law in 1978, employers have increasingly moved to this account because it is more cost-effective for them compared to pensions. With the right combination of employee contributions plus employer's match (if offered), market conditions, and time horizon, your plan appreciates to a future retirement balance that you aim toward well in advance, assuming that it will then provide for your retirement for at least twenty to thirty years.

I prefer the 401(k) retirement model to pensions because it offers you more freedom to make investment choices with your hard-earned money and to allocate those funds so you can meet your retirement goals based on your age, risk tolerance, and investing horizon. Additionally, the 401(k) also provides you with greater career mobility. You need not be tied down to one employer for life—you can roll over 401(k)s from employer to employer with considerable ease. In contrast, with pensions, the payout depended on how long someone worked at a company, which limited freedom of mobility between jobs and careers if one banked on a hefty pension at retirement.

But with this shift to 401(k)s also comes the imperative for you to take on more accountability for your own retirement planning and investing—and that's the hard part. We live in a world obsessed with conspicuous consumption and the flawed ideal to keep up with the Joneses. As a result, far too many people focus disproportionately on spending their hard-earned income today versus saving, investing, and creating wealth for retirement. Therefore, in my opinion, it is even more important for you to cultivate the confidence and competency it takes to ensure that you are financially literate and retirement ready.

The reality is that saving and investing is challenging for the general population, but on the plus side, the government has given your employer the option to provide you with a tax-advantaged means to

Pension	401(k)
What is it?	
A defined-benefit plan. These are more common in the public sector and no longer mainstream in the private sector.	A defined-contribution plan. These are the most common retirement plans today in the private sector.
Who is responsible for funding the plan?	
The employer provides contributions to the pension fund on an employee's behalf for guaranteed future income upon retirement.	You fund the 401(k) plan with portions of your pay, called "salary deferrals." You choose how much you want to contribute.
How does one receive retirement income?	
Pension benefits are determined by one's age, length of employment, and salary history. The employer provides a defined income every pay period from retirement until death.	Your account balance is affected by investment returns. Upon retirement, you withdraw funds from the account for income. The generally accepted advice is to withdraw no more than 4% each year.

Figure 1: Pension versus 401(k) comparison

achieve your retirement goals. But it's up to you to take advantage of this benefit. Today, when retirement is more dependent on your sensible actions and investment decisions, nothing could be more imperative than recognizing that DIY investing requires three primary ingredients:

1. **Internalizing the right financial values**
2. **Cultivating self-education**
3. **Acting now and adjusting later**[37]

Values matter the most

First, what are values? Values are the core of what you consider to be meaningful (or not) in your life. They, therefore, guide your thoughts, feelings, and actions toward what, how, and why you invest. While words like "discipline" and "accountability" or phrases like "financial literacy" and "fiscal responsibility" may on the surface seem like mere jargon, they constitute the very essence of the driving force that will guide you in prioritizing saving and investing for your future over spending all your income today.

DIY investing rests on what values you hold. Values are fairly abstract concepts that can be expressed in a single word or phrase. Some, but certainly not all, of the core values that I believe lead to successful DIY investing include the following:

- **Financial literacy**
- **Fiscal responsibility**
- **Self-discipline and accountability**
- **Long-term orientation**

Not until you emphasize values such as these, which aim your mindset and behavior toward investing goals, will you be ready to fully appreciate the next steps of this book. With them, you are more likely to follow through on building your DIY capabilities. When you value your future self (or your future descendants) who may benefit from the millions you'll make by retirement, then my five steps will be very useful to you. When you emphasize these values, you'll begin to think about your future. You'll feel a desire to provide for it, and so you'll begin to take the right steps to do so.

And since you've picked this book up, you're in the right direction so far, and so I encourage you to continue taking initiative here. I encourage you to cultivate an enriched value set that will lead you firmly down the path to broader investing and retirement-planning success. Remember: values take precedence over everything—even money.[38]

Build your DIY investing knowledge...for free!

Second, knowledge is power, right? That is certainly the case with DIY investing. To reach your retirement goals, you will need a solid foundation of investing knowledge that you can lean on to jump-start your 401(k). A great place to start your self-education is in a personal-finance course, most likely online. A personal-finance course wasn't mandatory at the University of Illinois at Urbana-Champaign, where I went to college, or, even more amazingly, for my degree program— which was economics.

Instead, I had to elect to take such a course. I enjoyed my economic studies; I listened with great attention to the theoretical models that predicted how consumers made decisions around saving versus consuming. But how could I apply that knowledge for my own benefit? It wasn't until the last semester of my senior year that I found the answer in a personal-wealth-management course. I can attest that it was the most valuable course I've ever taken to illuminate and inspire me to start investing right away. And, even better, after only a semester, I was competent enough to get started.

Whether you went to college or not (or are still there), your opportunities for 401(k) self-learning are abundant. (Learning doesn't stop after college, anyway—it is a lifelong process.) Investing today is more accessible than ever before with such resources that you can take advantage to further your self-learning from here. Your plan may offer free digital resources and tools to help you self-manage—make sure to check it out.

There are additional digital resources available too. Financial blogs are an excellent source of free information about investing basics, retirement accounts, living frugally, and overall how-tos for the DIY investor. Blogs are a great way to get others' perspectives on what has and has not worked for them as well as to get their recommendations. Individuals (like me!) and institutions alike have blogs.[39] And online personal-finance courses are fantastic because you can access them from the comfort of your home. They are often free. Last, use retirement calculators to see how much money you'll need to save up. (See also the recommended resources at the end of the book as well as an appendix on how to replicate all the cases in Microsoft Excel.[40])

Here are three digital resources that you can use to get started today:

1. **Free online personal-finance courses**
   o   CNN Money: Money 101
   o   Investopedia: Investing 101

2. **Online personal-finance and investing blogs**
   o The DIY Millionaire
   o Vanguard Blog
3. **Free retirement-income calculators**
   o Vanguard Retirement Income Calculator
   o CNN Money Retirement Calculator

Act now and adjust later

Third, time is your most precious asset when it comes to investing, and it works even better for you when you are investing for a retirement thirty to forty years away. You know the saying, "time is money." Each year you procrastinate investing while you are in your twenties and thirties costs you more and more in forgone earnings. Let's take a look at the years right out of college up to age thirty-five at the increasing amount of earnings you lose out on each year that you postpone 401(k) investing. (We visited this concept earlier with the examples of Eve and Adam. This example assumes Eve waited and the earnings forgone are derived from the variables from DIY 401(k) Math, Case 1.)

Age	Earnings forgone not investing
22	$203.83
23	$650.68
24	$1,134.70
25	$1,658.96
26	$2,226.81
27	$2,841.89
28	$3,508.11
29	$4,229.73
30	$5,011.35
31	$5,857.97
32	$6,775.00
33	$7,768.27
34	$8,844.14
35	$10,009.47

Figure 2: Cost of waiting to invest until age thirty-five

So how much money do you lose if you wait until age thirty-five to invest instead of starting promptly at age twenty-two? If you were to add up the earnings forgone from age twenty-two to thirty-five, you get

$60,720.91 lost by waiting to invest. And so we see that procrastination is costly. It is the opportunity cost of not investing. The cost becomes more substantial each year that you wait, since you have less time to invest. It's even more imperative, therefore, to become a DIY investor as soon as possible!

By now, you know that it takes the right values and education to cultivate your DIY investing mentality and capabilities. Once you have those, you are ready to start. You might feel overwhelmed and overloaded with information, but it is important to sift through the noise on investing out there and get started on your DIY investing journey now. At least get the investing process in motion. You can adjust and improve as you go along. The remainder of this book will walk you through getting started and how to sustain success as you strike it out on your own with your 401(k).[41]

Summary

This chapter was about Step 1 on your way from millennial to millionaire: becoming a DIY investor and taking ownership of your 401(k). You will need retirement income, and today, millennials must become DIY investors to reach their goals, because companies no longer offer old-style defined-benefit plans. You need to know the basics of how your 401(k) works and to acquire the necessary ingredients of a DIY investor: the right values, financial self-education, and taking action now.

Step 1 Takeaways

- Pensions are outdated and are no longer a mainstream corporate retirement-plan option.
- A 401(k) is today's most common method of retirement saving because it is cost-effective for your employer and flexible for you.
- A 401(k) is a tax-advantaged investment account used to save for retirement.
- If an employer offers a 401(k) plan, its employees all may invest in it after any enrollment-restriction period or minimum-age requirement.

- You contribute to a 401(k) from your take-home pay through salary deferrals, and your employer may provide a matching contribution.
- A DIY investor must possess three ingredients:
  o The right financial values
  o Self-education
  o Action now (and adjustment later)
- The values that underlie 401(k) investing are financial literacy and fiscal responsibility, along with self-discipline and a long-term orientation.
- Financial self-education is key to learning 401(k) basics and about investing in general, and you can learn by taking a personal-finance course online, reading personal-finance blogs, and using free retirement-income calculators.
- Time is your most important asset when it comes to investing, so don't procrastinate. Act now!

STEP 2

How much to save for retirement

What kind of retirement do you want?

Investing—and in 401(k)s in particular—is inherently a very personal endeavor. It's as much psychology as it is finance. It requires you to take stock of your priorities and your values and to decide what actions to take now—what is the importance of your future savings versus consumption today? In fact, retirement may mean something very different for you compared to what it means for your colleague, your best friend, your mom and dad, or even for your significant other. It's completely subjective.

My goal is to help you not just see beyond the black-and-white numbers associated with saving for retirement but also investigate and appreciate the vision you have for yourself in the far future. In Step 2, you will be asked to think about what retirement means to you. Start to think now of what you want to do when you reach age sixty-seven. Once we have gained a deeper appreciation of the subjectivity of retirement, we will move onto a more objective discussion of how to start saving now. Yes, maybe you're challenged with student-loan debt, and other financial constraints, but I'll take you step-by-step on how to start saving small and how to incrementally improve from there.

To begin with, by now you know that 401(k) investing is for producing retirement income. Sounds straightforward enough: you contribute to your 401(k) plan every pay period, the account grows tax-free if it's a Roth or tax-deferred if it's traditional through the effect of compounding, and then when you retire, you withdraw funds as your income every year. But what will you use that income for when you retire at age sixty-seven?

Pause for a moment and contemplate what you would do with that money. For some, the word "retirement" conjures up imagery of golfing all day and spending one's hard-earned money on luxuries like a nice condo in Florida or Arizona (like so many of my mom's friends!) and traveling to exotic countries. For others, the imagery may lean to the more ordinary, such as volunteering in one's own town or working just a part-time gig. For some, retirement may simply mean staying put in the house one has already lived in for thirty or more years. Hopefully by then, the mortgage has been paid off!

Surely, retirement isn't a one-size-fits-all model of postemployment life. It's not just about the money you save; it's about the lifestyle you want at that time. While I will certainly teach you the techniques and tools you need to move from a millennial to a millionaire, I can't define what being a millionaire in retirement means for you. It's up to you to contemplate what purpose that million-dollar-plus wealth will serve you.

No matter how much you accumulate, you know that money for the sake of money won't guarantee you any more satisfaction in retirement than you have today. I'm inspired by a saying that goes, "Who is rich? One who is satisfied with his lot."[42] In other words, your happiness comes from a contented state of mind, not simply from a state of material wealth. Money is a means, and not an end. On the other hand, who is not rich? Maybe it's those who are constantly in the pursuit of more money simply for its own sake. Money without a purpose doesn't benefit you or anyone else. So think: How are you going to use your money? What's the lifestyle you want in retirement?

To illustrate this question, let's revisit our friend Eve. She accumulated $2,287,499.42 (see DIY 401(k) Math, Case 1), which will certainly help her pay her bills in retirement. But what else? Let's say you truly love your occupation. Why stop just because you reach retirement age? My grandfather retired from his job as a professor at the University of Chicago at the age of seventy, but he continued to teach and write. If you truly love your hometown and have a great social network, why move somewhere where you are a stranger and away from your loved ones? Of course, the opposite holds as well—if you truly detest your occupation or hometown, then make a change!

What does current research say about millennials conceptions of retirement? Recent data shows that millennials don't see retirement as a sudden exit from the workforce or a decrease in productivity. On the contrary, they want to stay active in their retirement years. They want a steady "phased transition" away from their nine-to-five jobs and into more personally meaningful work and leisure. Here are some statistics:

- Forty-four percent want a phased retirement transition to work with reduced hours and more meaning.[43]
- Seventy percent want to spend their retirements traveling.[44]
- Sixty-three percent cited wanting to spend more time with family and friends.[45]
- Twenty-four percent expressed an interest in more volunteer work.[46]
- Thirty-four percent want to keep working for enjoyment and to stay engaged and active.[47]

So you see from these indicators that millennials already view retirement as so much more as a subjective experience than simply just about how much they save in total. Today, the data implies that it is becoming a mixture of meaningful work and leisure activities. Even from the very beginning of your retirement planning, think about what retirement really means to you. That can help you decide how much you'll need to save over the next thirty to forty years to sustain your vision for a purposeful retirement.

Start to save for retirement now!

Studies show that 47 percent of millennials believe that they need to retire with a million dollars in hand.[48] This amount seems to stick in the popular imagination. My whole life, the million-dollar mark has been the gold standard of measuring that someone is "rich." Oddly enough, millennials' retirement targets are almost no different from those of baby boomers (those born between 1946 and 1964).[49] However, a dollar isn't always worth the same at different points in time. By the time millennials retire (circa 2040–2060), even a million will not be enough. In 1987 dollars, that amount would have bought twice as much as it does today, and back in 1929, right before the Great Depression, today's million could have bought fourteen times what it would buy now.

Why is this important? Look at the trend. The buying power of money was higher per dollar in the past, and it is likely to be worth less in the future—even less so in the far-off future when millennials retire. This means that you need to save and invest enough to replace your work income *and* account for inflationary pressures to stay at the same quality of life. Dedicated savings and investing boost your 401(k) balance, but inflation is the invisible cost that eats away at it year by year.

In this section, I'll show you an incremental way to save so that you can live the retirement lifestyle you envision for yourself. First, in general, the financial professional community promotes a common rule of thumb that for retirement, you should save 10–15 percent of your current income. But that rate isn't always doable at first, so let's start small and work our way up.

No matter where you start, I will repeat that it's incredibly important to start saving as soon as possible. I know that retirement may not be on your mind when you are young, given that it's so far away, but small amounts today lead to big earnings in the far future. (Additionally, you may have student-loan debt that you're not sure how to balance against the demands of saving for retirement. But the reality is that you have to.)

Get started now:

1. **Contribute at least your employer's matching amount.**
2. **At the same time, pay down student loans.**

After we discuss these action steps, we'll look at tips on how to incrementally move up to saving 10–15 percent of your salary.

Contribute at least your employer's match

The very first thing to do is to contribute to your 401(k) at least the amount that your employer will match. Eve's employer matches 100 percent of the first 4 percent of eligible pay. (This is, as noted, just an example, because every employer is different, and some don't match at all.) The point here is that when you contribute up to your employer's match, you make a 100 percent return on your investment. It's truly free money—and you can't afford not to take it. Nowhere else—not in any bank's savings or checking account or in any taxable or nontaxable investment account—will you get as great a deal as an employer's matching contribution. Take advantage of it right now.

Let's say that Eve contributed up to only the employer's match rather than the typical millennial 7 percent. How much would she have by the time she reached age sixty-seven? $1,663,635.94! So even with a flat $47,000 salary for the rest of her career, she is still a millionaire at retirement—saving only 4 percent of her salary! This demonstrates how small amounts invested when you are young grow exponentially over time, when additionally powered by an employer's matching contribution.

There's a downside, however, if you don't contribute up to the employer's match—you lose free money. Think of the employer's match as the minimum that you must contribute. In Eve's case, how much free money would she lose if she put absolutely nothing (0 percent) in her 401(k) over the forty-five years of her entire career? Shockingly, she would have lost out on $831,817.97 of free money![50]

Clearly, letting so much free money go is a suboptimal decision that you must avoid as you start to invest in your 401(k). You can see that contributing at least the company's match will propel you far faster down your path to a much more lucrative retirement portfolio. Where else would you ever get that much free money? Don't lose out on the opportunity if you have it!

Keep in mind that each employer has their own matching schedule. In Eve's case, it's fairly straightforward—it's 100 percent up to the first 4 percent of eligible pay. You *might* see more involved schedules—50 percent up to the first 6 percent of eligible pay, in which case you truly get 3 percent (= 6 × .50). Or something more complex, such as 100 percent up to the first 3 percent, plus 50 percent of the next 3 percent of eligible pay, for a total matching contribution of 4.5 percent (= (3 × 1.0) + (3 × .50)). Make sure you know what your employer's matching contribution schedule looks like (if offered).

Don't get an employer's match? If you don't, you could still retire a millionaire, even without the free money you get with a match. If you start at 5 percent even on a $47,000 salary at age twenty-two, you would retire a millionaire. (To check the math, go to Case 1 in DIY 401(k) Math and replicate those steps, inputting $2,350 (= .05 × $47,000) into *pmt* in your Excel formula.) On the positive side, if you really can't do that and need to start below that rate, then you aren't losing out on any free money. Still, strive to achieve for at least a 5 percent contribution rate to start.

How to pay off student debt and save for retirement

Paying down student debt is a real millennial concern. But I don't want that to stop you from saving in your 401(k). You'll need to balance both. I graduated from the University of Illinois in 2010 with around $25,000 in student debt, with a $50,000 salary. I knew that I wanted to eliminate this as soon as possible and save in my 401(k), so I made both financial priorities. As a result, I paid back my student loans in four years.

The conversation on student debt repayment is rich, and I won't try to go into all the details here. My goal is to equip you with my own personal strategies that helped me to pay them down in a relatively short time window as well as save in my 401(k). However, I must emphasize that you should not, under any circumstance, try to defer (or even avoid) paying your student debt! The interest on the loan that you borrowed will simply continue to grow and compound, leaving you with even more to pay off later.

Here are my personal tips to help pay down your debt faster as well as save in your 401(k):

1. **Choose a student-loan repayment plan immediately after graduation that works best for your financial situation**. The US government offers you a menu of repayment plans to choose from that best meet your financial needs. Take time to review which option may work best for you. For example, the Standard Repayment Plan gives you up to ten years to repay the student loans and

payments are a fixed amount. I was on the standard plan. There are also a couple of types of income-driven repayment plans that you can choose, depending on eligibility.[51]

2. **Estimate your monthly loan repayment amount and pay more than that amount if you can.** With the Standard Repayment Plan, your plan will estimate how much you should pay each month to pay off the entirety of your student loans within ten years. For example, the average four-year public-loan amount is around $26,946, which translates to $272/month in payments.[52] Pay this amount, or even better try to pay more if you can.

3. **Apply any signing bonus and/or year-end bonus to your student-loan payments.** One way that helped me pay off my student loans fast was I applied my signing bonus and any subsequent yearly bonuses to paying the loans. It may be tempting to spend that money, but don't. Don't get either of those? Then apply your tax-return refund to your student-loan repayment. In fact, your tax refund may be higher than normal as you begin to work because you may qualify to deduct up to $2,500 in student-loan interest from your annual gross income.[53]

Keep retirement savings top of mind too. Live within your means today to accomplish both. As we talked about, at least start with contributing up to your employer's match (or 5 percent if not offered one). Truthfully, this may mean that you will need to sacrifice certain luxuries today. But nevertheless, identify those expenses you can cut out to balance these two priorities to live frugally. Also, after college I happen to get a job in Richmond, Virginia, that had a lower cost of living than where I live now, Chicago. This move helped me lower my housing expenses, which allowed me to earmark even more money to pay down my student loans.

Tips to help you achieve a 10–15 percent savings rate

Once you have gotten a good handle on paying down your student debt and you're saving at least the employer's match (or at least 5 percent), you will want to work up toward saving 10–15 percent of your pay over time to ensure a secure and comfortable retirement. You'll see that getting there incrementally over time will be a lot easier than doing it all at once. Go slow to go fast here.

Here are three tips to achieve this:

1. **Sign up for your 401(k) plan's annual increase program.** Your employer may offer an annual increase program you can opt in to. Some plans let you pick a future increase date and percentage at the time you enroll. For example, you may be contributing 4 percent today to meet your company's match but elect to increase that by at least 1 percent more each year every July 1. Clearly, you'll be at a 10 percent rate automatically after six years—and at 15 percent rate after eleven years—with the firm and benefitting more from compounding as you go.

2. **Increase your contribution rate with every raise.** An easy way to increase your contribution rate is to do it by whatever amount of raise you receive. Let's say you get a 1 or 2 percent raise each year—don't spend that increase but add those extra dollars into your 401(k) savings by manually increasing your contribution rate equal to the raise amount. You'll be saving more but won't feel it at all!

3. **Just make it a goal.** Maybe your plan doesn't offer an annual increase program, or shoot, you don't get a raise. In that case, just making it a personal goal to stretch yourself is half the battle. You know those resolutions you make for New Year's? Make it a resolution to incrementally get up to 10–15 percent over time. And if you write that goal down on paper, you're more likely to follow through!

Why saving 10–15 percent of your annual salary is crucial

Personal growth is an important element to a DIY investor, and once you have made saving at least the company's match and paying down student loans a *habit*, you'll want to continue to stretch your savings capabilities—and to strive to save 10–15 percent. Our friend Eve started by investing 7 percent of her pay, which is already more than her company's match.

She's already ahead of the game compared to most in her generation. How much further ahead would she be if she began to incrementally work up to saving 10–15 percent of her salary each year?

Maybe you noticed that I haven't asked you to calculate how much money you will need in retirement or how much of your salary do you need to replace in the far future. The truth of the matter is that those exercises are too time-consuming and of little value because you can't really estimate how much you will need in retirement. However, saving up to 10–15 percent can ensure you're not left empty handed when you hit retirement, and saving a little bit more today, when you are young, will yield exponentially higher results by your retirement years, leaving you with more money to enjoy on yourself then.

So how much more would Eve amass if she stretched herself to save 10–15 percent? Assuming an 8 percent return on investment over Eve's working years, let's see how much more she'd have at retirement if she contributed 10 or 15 percent of her salary instead of just meeting the employer's match or the average millennial contribution rate.[54]

Eve contributes	Her future 401(k) balance is
4% of income (meeting the employer's match)	$1,663,635.94
7% (the average millennial contribution rate)	$2,287,499.42
10%	$2,911,362.89
15%	$3,951,135.36

Figure 3: Relationship between contribution rate and future 401(k) balance

Wow! Quite the difference between the 7 percent up until the 15 percent contribution rate. It's obvious that as contributions increase, the future value of the 401(k) account increases as well—there is a direct relationship. And, of course, if you can contribute more than the 10–15 percent guideline, that's even better for your future retirement balance.[55] How does the account value rise so much at higher savings rates?

1. **More contribution adds more principal every pay period to your account.** To illustrate, 7 percent of $47,000 is $3,290 a year, but a

10 percent contribution is $4,700 a year. So for roughly $117.50 more each month (maybe the cost of a *latte* per day!), you can expect a $623,863.47 increase (for a final value of $2,911,362.89 instead of $2,287,499.42) in your future 401(k)! Or a 15 percent contribution is $7,050 a year. The difference between 7 percent is $313.33 more each month. That's about $10/day—the cost of *eating out* for lunch! Brown-bag it to work, and you can expect a $1,663,635.94 increase in your retirement savings!

2. **Your employer's match gives your 401(k) the extra kick it needs, effectively increasing your savings rate.** In this example, Eve's employer also matches 100 percent of the first 4 percent of eligible pay. Your annual contribution is then bumped up an extra $1,880 each pay period—that's free money! So while you save 10 percent of your own money, your actual savings rate is 14 percent, and 19 percent when you save 15 percent!

3. **The power of compounding increases and accelerates 401(k) growth with a higher contribution rate.** Let's assume that your 401(k) is invested in the stock market and averaging an 8 percent annual return. Your increased contributions are making more in earnings each year, which then make even more money on themselves over time. With the power of compounding, a little difference today can add a whole lot to your 401(k) portfolio tomorrow.

You may say that at your young age, this is a big ask, because you may have student loans, a car loan, or a mortgage to pay down. But if you can save more, do it. Use the tactics discussed above to set goals to get to this savings rate over time.

How to budget like a millionaire to put this all into practice

All right, I've just thrown a lot at you about how much to save for retirement, why you need to pay down student debt and how to incrementally save up to 10–15 percent of your salary. To actualize all of this, you need to start with a budget. A budget is a methodical way to know what money is coming in (income) and what money is going out (expenses and savings). We know you have to start saving for retirement now and you have student loans, but you'll probably have other financial demands as well to account for, such as housing expenses, an auto loan, and money to spend for entertainment.

There are many budgeting methods out there, but the simplest method that you can get started with right now to account for 401(k) saving, paying down student debt and managing additional finances is *percentage budgeting*. With this approach, you allocate a percentage of your *net income* to the budgeting categories of your choosing. Net income is your pay after income taxes and 401(k) contributions are subtracted.

First, prioritize 401(k) savings. At first, allot the percentage amount of your employer's match, and then move up to a max 15 percent of your salary for retirement savings depending on where you are in your incremental saving. This amount will be automatically deducted from your gross pay.

Second, housing is going to be your biggest *net* pay expense. For those of you who live in New York City and San Francisco, I'm sure you're terribly aware of this! Nonetheless, you should spend no more than 35 percent of net income on rent, utilities, and insurance—or even on a mortgage if you own your residence.

Third, know how much your monthly student loan payment is and calculate that as a percentage of net income. In this case, the standard repayment program gives you ten years to pay off student loans, and if you went to a public four-year university the average student debt is $26,946, which translates to $272/month in payments. Let's use this as our working assumption in the budget example below.

Fourth, the remaining percentage is yours that you can use to spend on miscellaneous expenses, such as a car loan, and those nights you just want to have fun with your friends. This category can be around 50 percent of net pay. Other spending categories to consider are cable/internet, dining out, travel/vacation, healthcare/medical, groceries, and personal care expenses. Or, even better, start to contribute to an emergency fund to save for life's unexpected expenses.

Example millennial budget

Let's say you make $47,000 per year, like our friends Eve and Adam. This translates roughly to $3,917 per month (= $47,000/12). With this income, you are in the 25 percent federal marginal tax bracket.[56] And assume you incrementally raised your 401(k) contribution rate to 15 percent. (I ignore state income tax for simplicity.)

Gross pay tax & deductions

- Gross pay: $3,917
- Tax (25%): $979 (= $3,917 × .25)
- 401(k) contribution (max 15%): $588 (= $3,917 × .15)
- Net pay: $2,350 (= $3,917 − $979 − $588)

So you have your net pay to work with your monthly budget.

Net pay budget

- Housing (35%): $822 (= $2,350 × .35)
- Student debt (12%): $272
- Remaining expenses (53%): $1,256 (= $2,350 − $822 − $272)

Interpreting the budget

Let's look at what this budget means to how you can spend on those categories:

1. **Retirement.** You should save a maximum amount of $588/month in your 401(k). The neat observation here is that see how manageable 15 percent of your gross pay seems in the grand scheme of things? (Of note, this example is after-tax, but for practical budgeting purposes, it makes little difference if you were contributing to a traditional or Roth at a $47,000 annual salary, as will be explained in the next chapter on the two 401(k) accounts.)
2. **Housing.** You can spend a maximum of $822/month on rent, utilities, and insurance. That may mean you can't afford to live

in the new commercial high-rise complex, with all the fancy amenities and rooftop pool! Instead you may need to live in a cheaper neighborhood, live in a smaller space, or even bunk up with roommates—or many. You can live in more luxurious living conditions once you get your finances in shape and are a bit older.

3. **Student debt.** Calculate your monthly payment and bake the amount into your net pay budget. In this example, make sure to pay $272/month or more.

4. **Remainder.** You now have $1,256 remaining in your budget. How can you allocate this money? First, you can use this amount to increase your student loan payments. Second, allocate it towards additional expenses, such as a car loan, dining out, cable/internet, etc. Or you can begin to use this amount to open a high-yield savings account to use as an emergency fund. Just remember, that your remaining expenses shouldn't exceed $1,256/month.

Want to go the extra step and open an emergency fund? If you choose to do so, strive first to save at least $1,000 for unexpected expenses, and then work up to saving 3 to 9 months' worth of income. Saving in an emergency fund can take a year's worth or more of saving. If you want to first achieve $1,000 in one year, set a monthly goal to set aside around $83/month (= $1,000/12). Once you hit $1,000, set another goal to save 3 months' worth of expenses, and plan to save accordingly each month until you reach your goal. And then do the same for 6 months, and then 9 months. Start small!

You may be thinking, "Are you saying that even on $47,000 per year, I can afford up to 15 percent on 401(k) savings, 35 percent on housing, pay down my student loans, and still be left with $1,256 each month?" Yes, I am! See how with a budget you get an orderly and precise picture on where your money is coming from and where it's going?

And as you advance in your budgeting, find new and improved ways to cut out excesses, such as buying coffee in the morning, eating out for lunch at work every day, and paying for expensive gym memberships and too much for your cable bill, just to name a few. In sum, constantly look to slim down these costs in your budget![57]

Caution: What you see in the future isn't what you always get

So far in our discussion, we have used an 8 percent annual return on investment as an example rate over the long term. That is because the S&P 500, a barometer of the stock market's performance, has produced that rate of return over time (including the effects of market gains and losses as well as reinvested dividends).[58] There are three inputs that go into growing your 401(k): your employee contributions (plus any employer's match), your investing time horizon, and your portfolio's investment return. But appearances can be deceiving. The fact is that the 401(k) balance that you see in the future will be impacted by not only compounding but also inflation. These processes counteract. With the first, we gain, but with the second, we lose ground.

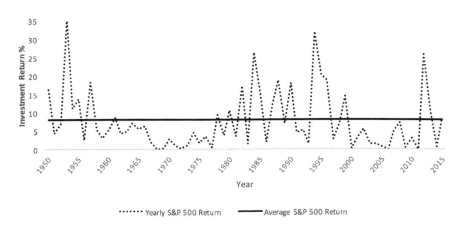

Figure 4: Stock market return chart (1950–2016)
Source: Data is from Yahoo! Finance. Graph is my own.

Compounding accelerates earnings growth

First, let's review the concept of compounding in more detail here. Compounding accelerates earnings growth as relatively small contributions grow into larger sums over the long term. Your contributions to your 401(k) from your salary build your investment principal. Your principal appreciates over time through stock market gains and income returns (i.e., reinvested dividends), called "earnings." The percentage of investment return measures the earnings that the principal receives. Compound interest is when those earnings make even more money on themselves.

Compound interest accrues over long periods through two necessary ingredients: the stock market's investment return (i.e., an 8 percent average) and the investing time horizon (i.e., forty-five years or so) that you have to invest. The more you have of both ingredients, the higher your 401(k) account balance will be when you retire. Let's look at an example.

Assume you contribute a lump sum of $1,000 to your 401(k) on December 31. This $1,000 is the principal. Then, by the end of year 1— next December 31—the stock market has risen by 8 percent, and so you now have $1,080 (= $1,000 × 1.08). The $80 (= $1,080 – $1,000) is your earnings. At the end of year 2, the market has risen another 8 percent, but you don't just get another 8 percent on your original lump sum of $1,000. You get 8 percent on $1,080, giving you a total of $1,166.40 (= $1,080 × 1.08). The $86.40 (= $1,166.40 – $1,080) is your compounded earnings. The interest accumulated on the interest is called "compound interest."

What's more, at the end of twenty years, your initial $1,000, without any further contributions to the original principal, will grow to $4,660.96, and at the end of forty-five years, it will rise to $31,920.45—if an investment return of 8 percent continues every year. Compounding is the accumulative process of earning compound interest on your initial principal and on the accrued earnings over time.

Year	Amount
0	$1,000.00
1	$1,080.00
2	$1,166.40
3	$1,259.71
4	$1,360.49
5	$1,469.33
20	$4,660.96
45	$31,920.45

Figure 5: Compounding of $1,000 over forty-five years at 8 percent investment return

As we see in the chart above, there is a direct correlation between the long-term investment return and the amount that $1,000 will produce by the end of forty-five years. The higher the return, the more $1,000 grows into. The power of compounding similarly keeps your 401(k) portfolio growing, even exponentially, into the millions over a thirty- or forty-year plus career.

Compounding isn't easy mental math, so a quick shortcut for calculating how long it will take your money to double is the "rule of 72." It tells you how many years are required to double your money given a certain investment return. For example, since the average stock market investment return is 8 percent, you might expect to double your 401(k) investments every nine years (= 72/8). Over a forty-five-year span of investing, therefore, your money could double exactly five times.[59] But again, even though the stock market produces 8 percent over the long term, remember that past performance is not a guarantee of future returns. This is a rule of thumb to get an estimate of future earnings. Any investment can result in partial or complete loss of principal.

Inflation brings earnings down

Now let's look at the process of inflation. It is one reason that what you see in the future isn't what you get. The S&P 500's 8 percent investment return is called the nominal rate of return. It is nominal because it doesn't take inflation into consideration. Whereas compounding is the rate at which your money grows over time, inflation is the rate at which your money depreciates over time. This is a key distinction. The difference between the nominal rate and inflation is called the real rate of return, which reflects the purchasing power that your money will possess in the future.

Therefore, the real rate of return = nominal rate of return − inflation. Inflation varies from year to year, with the annual rate rising to a high of 13.5 percent in 1980 to its lowest point of −0.1 percent (i.e., *de*flation) in 2009, right after the Great Recession. Based on data from the Bureau of Labor Statistics,[60] the inflation rate over the long term (1950–2016) has stabilized to around 3.5 percent.

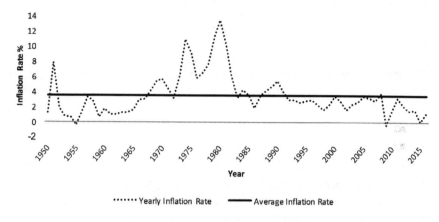

Figure 6: Inflation rate chart (1950–2016)
Source: Data is from the Bureau of Labor Statistics. Graph is my own.

So while Eve started investing 7 percent of her income, and we saw how much her account would be had she invested 10–15 percent, what are the implications of inflation on her future 401(k) balance? In other words, when we add inflation into the equation, how much is her 401(k) worth at various contribution rates over the long term? Let's take a look at what purchasing power her 401(k) will have after forty-five years.[61]

Eve contributes	Her 401(k) real balance is
4% of her income (meeting the employer's match)	$548,363.53
7% (average millennial contribution rate)	$753,999.86
10%	$959,636.18
15%	$1,302,363.39

Figure 7: Relationship between contribution rate and real 401(k) balance

Were you surprised that her 7 percent contribution rate doesn't even get the balance to a million dollars? Only when she contributes up to 15 percent does the real value exceed a million dollars. Yes—in forty-five years, her 401(k) with a 15 percent contribution rate will have the purchasing power of today's $1,302,363.39. In sum, you must take inflation into consideration when you are doing retirement planning.

What key lessons can you learn here about inflation's impact on your 401(k) balance over the long term?

1. **Inflation dramatically decreases purchasing power over the long term.** The most striking observation here is that inflation dramatically decreases purchasing power, and it gets more intense as the balance rises. For example, if Eve contributes 15 percent of her income, inflation takes away $2,648,771.97 (= $3,951,135.36 – $1,302,363.39) in purchasing power. Now, let me clarify that when Eve retires, her 401(k) account will show a statement balance of $3,951,135.36, but inflation means that this amount will only buy what $1,302,363.39 buys today. Inflation took millions in purchasing power away!

2. **You need to save as much as you can to overcome losses from inflation, working to incrementally save at least 15 percent of your pay each year.** The second lesson is it is even more clear and imperative that you should contribute as much and as early as you can to accrue the benefits of compounding. In fact, if you don't save at least the average inflation rate (3.5 percent), you'll end up with a negative real 401(k) balance after forty-five years of investing. To overcome this challenge, graduate your savings rate to higher levels over time, at or even above 15 percent of your income.

Summary

This chapter was Step 2 on your way from millennial to millionaire and was about defining your retirement goals. You defined how much you need in retirement for comfortable living. We discussed the qualitative and quantitative factors of calculating retirement needs, and these are very personal. We covered a graduated model for increasing your contribution rate over time to meet your retirement goals. The recommendation is to save 10–15 percent of your annual salary. We also illustrated how compounding increases your earnings over time and also how inflation significantly decreases the buying power of your 401(k) portfolio.

Step 2 Takeaways

- Your retirement goal is more than just a number. It has a subjective quality that only you can define.
- A million dollars no longer defines sufficient wealth for an expected twenty- to thirty-year retirement.
- You should start to save as early as possible:
  - First, contribute up to your employer's match to get free money (or at least 5 percent if not offered a match).
  - At the same time, pay down student debt.
  - Move up to saving 10–15 percent of your salary, using my tips on increasing your contributions over time.
- Use percentage budgeting for net income (after taxes and 401(k) contributions) to account for where your money is coming from and where your money is going.
- Stock market gains appreciate your 401(k) balance through compounding (as well as reinvested dividends) over the long term.
- Past performance isn't a guarantee of future returns, but the stock market's return on investment has averaged around 8 percent over the long term.
- Inflation depreciates your 401(k) balance, reducing purchasing power in the future.
- Inflation has averaged around 3.5 percent over the long term.
- The real rate of return on your retirement portfolio is the nominal rate of return minus the rate of inflation.
- Save as much as you can, eventually at or more than 15 percent, to beat inflation.

STEP 3

Choose the right 401(k) account option

The two flavors of the 401(k) you need to know

A nswer this question: Do you want to be taxed on your contributions when you make withdrawals during retirement, or do you want to be taxed now, while you are working?

Your response to this will give you a sense of which 401(k) account may work best for you. Your choice depends on when you want the tax treatment to kick in. Of note, however, not all employers offer the Roth 401(k) option. If that is the case, you must select the traditional 401(k). But if your employer does offer it, read on.

In Step 3, we will uncover in more detail the differences between these two accounts. We will then go over a general framework on how to choose which account is best suited for your financial outlook and current versus expected tax situation. Lastly, we will go over some features you may encounter in your plan, such as a Roth in-plan conversion, as well as walk through a quick digest on non-401(k) salary-deferral plans.

The traditional versus Roth 401(k)

The Two Types of 401(k) Accounts

There are two types of 401(k) accounts: a traditional 401(k), also known as a pretax 401(k), and a Roth 401(k), if offered in your plan. The difference has to do with when you pay ordinary income taxes on the money. They are similar in that (1) they require withdrawals after age seventy and a half, (2) they are tax-advantaged retirement-savings vehicles, and (3) there are no income-limit restrictions, meaning that you can continue to earn more pay at your job and still contribute to either plan (up to the annual contribution limit). Also, if you leave your job or retire, both account types can be rolled out of the employer-sponsored plan and into an individual retirement account (IRA).

The Traditional 401(k) Account

In a traditional 401(k), you contribute money on a pretax basis—this means that taxes are not deducted from the amount you contribute. Your contributions are subtracted from your taxable income. In other words, contributing lowers your taxable income in the year you do it. This is a tax-deferred account, which means that you will pay ordinary income taxes on your contributions, any employer's matching contributions, and earnings on those contributions when you withdraw in retirement.

The Roth 401(k) Account

In a Roth 401(k), unlike the traditional, your contributions are made on an after-tax basis. This means that you pay ordinary income taxes on your contributions up front, while you are working, and so your contributions do not reduce your taxable income. However, your Roth earnings are withdrawn tax-free when you take money out of the account in retirement. (Note, however, that any employer's matches going into a Roth account are taxed like traditional contributions. They are made pretax, and you will pay tax on these withdrawals in retirement.)

Ordinarily, the conversation on choosing which account to pick rests on the contrast between what you currently pay in taxes compared to what you expect to pay in retirement. But other factors are at play as well. For example, you may want to save on taxes today through a traditional

401(k) and earmark the unpaid taxes for another savings account such as an emergency fund or an IRA to supplement your 401(k) retirement savings. Or you might prefer not to be bothered with income taxes when you retire. It's important to assess the different account types before you make your decision.

Impact on take-home pay

The options have different impacts on your take-home pay, because of their differing tax treatment. Let's look in on our friend Eve. She gets paid biweekly (twenty-six times each year). What is the impact on her take-home pay of contributing to a traditional 401(k) versus a Roth 401(k)? Her salary is $47,000, and she contributes 7 percent to her 401(k) each pay period; she is in the 25 percent marginal tax bracket.[62] (Note that the employer's match doesn't impact the calculation of her take-home pay.)

Traditional 401(k)	Roth 401(k)
Gross pay	**Gross pay**
$1,808 (= $47,000/26)	$1,808 (= $47,000/26)
Contribution	**Tax**
$127 (= $3,290/26)	$452 (= $1,808 × .25)
Pretax income	**Posttax income**
$1,681 (= $1,808 − $127)	$1,356 (= $1,808 − $452)
Tax	**Roth contribution**
$420 (= $1,681 × .25)	$127 (= $3,290/26)
Net pay	**Net pay**
$1,261 (= $1,681 − $420)	$1,229 (= $1,356 − $127)

Figure 8: Traditional versus Roth 401(k) effect on take-home pay

Three observations here:

1. **Net pay is higher when you select the traditional 401(k) compared to a Roth 401(k).** With a traditional 401(k), you are not taxed on the contribution amount each pay period. Instead, it is deducted from gross income before it is taxed. Therefore, with a traditional 401(k), you walk away each pay period with a higher net income than with a Roth 401(k).
2. **Tax savings from a traditional 401(k) are small at lower pay levels.** The savings that Eve receives each pay period is only $32 (= $1,261 − $1,229) with a traditional 401(k). For the entire year, she saves $823 (= $32 × 26).
3. *But* **tax savings from a traditional 401(k) increase at higher pay levels.** But if she made $120,000 a year, after many promotions from working diligently, and she incrementally worked up to save at least 15 percent of her annual pay, she'd save $194 per pay period, which would add up to $5,040 (= $194 × 26) each year. That's almost the maximum that Eve could put into an IRA to supplement her retirement investing alongside her traditional 401(k). (Of note, the 2017 annual maximum contribution limit to an IRA is $5,500.)

Next up, let's look at ways to decide which account best fits your financial situation. (The next section is more mathematics heavy, so you may want to skip to the section after it entitled, "Still can't decide what to choose? Read this!")

Choose either a traditional or a Roth 401(k)

You may have heard that you should opt for the Roth 401(k) because you are a young adult. This advice rests on a generalized set of assumptions about millennials' saving behaviors, investing time horizons, current tax situation, and future tax rates. Yes, the Roth 401(k) can be an ideal option for young adults who invest early. I myself contribute exclusively to a Roth. But it is not ideal for all young adults. I'll describe the key considerations for choosing which account is better for you.

To begin with, I can't stress enough that there is no one-size-fits-all model in investing. Take stock of your current financial situation, which includes your expected average lifetime salary, contribution rate, and current tax rate, and measure it against your expectations for the future. This is a challenging exercise because predicting the future is never certain. You can only reach a level of probability of what will happen. Attempting to predict what your future will look like in thirty, forty, or more years has a wide margin of error. Still, it is possible to make reasoned extrapolations about the future based on your current savings and tax situation.

The chart below outlines the key considerations you should factor in when deciding which 401(k) account is aligned best to your current situation and your expectations of the future. The top four considerations are as follows:

- Your *current tax rate*, which is derived from your average lifetime salary and tax liability before retirement
- Your expectations about your *future tax rate* in retirement, which is calculated from the expected withdrawals from your 401(k) balance
- Your *savings behavior*
- Your *investing time horizon*

Traditional 401(k)	Roth 401(k)
Contributions	**Contributions**
Come from pretax income, reducing gross income reported to the IRS.	Come from taxable income, not reducing gross income reported to the IRS.
Withdrawals after age fifty-nine and a half	**Withdrawals after age fifty-nine and a half**
Taxed at your ordinary income-tax rate.	Tax-free, provided your account is open at least five years. (Any employer's match money will be taxed.)
Current tax rate versus expected future rate	**Current tax rate versus expected future rate**
Traditional is more beneficial if your current income tax rate is higher than what you expect it to be at retirement.	Roth is more advantageous if your current income tax is lower than what you expect it to be at retirement.
Savings behavior	**Savings behavior**
More advantageous if your contribution rate is low, since you'll have a lower account balance at retirement, and thus your smaller withdrawals will come with a lower tax liability.	More beneficial if you save more (10–15%), because you'll have a higher account balance in retirement, and thus your higher withdrawals will come with a higher tax liability.
Investing horizon	**Investing horizon**
More beneficial if you start investing later in life, since you have less time to invest and grow your portfolio, which means you'll have a lower account balance.	More advantageous if you start investing promptly in your early to midtwenties, since you'll have more time on your side to invest and grow your portfolio.

Figure 9: Traditional 401(k) versus Roth 401(k) comparison

Why does the financial community usually recommend the Roth 401(k) for young-adult investors? It's because of the bold assumption that tax rates in the far future will be higher than they are today, placing a higher weight on that consideration. This assumption isn't altogether unsound. It's very possible that with the current extraordinary high level of national debt in the United States and with the current political establishment's reticence to pass reasonable tax legislation, forty-five years from now, the tax bill on future generations will be higher to finance an even bigger national debt. We can never be truly certain of future tax rates, though. Regardless, the other three considerations are just as important.

Let's demonstrate the difference between the traditional and Roth accounts with our pals Eve and Adam. (**Important note:** Here, I use today's federal tax rates,[63] since we can't really predict what they will be in the far future. I also ignore state income taxes for ease of analysis, as well as income taxes paid on the employer match money in a Roth.)

A traditional is good for late savers and tax savings today

Adam is thirty-five but is only getting started with his 401(k). But should he choose a traditional or Roth? He may benefit from a traditional 401(k) because he got a late start at investing. Let's see why that could be the case.[64]

Step 1. Determine your current tax rate and tax savings. Adam, as we've noted, makes the same $47,000 salary across his whole career. This puts him in the 25 percent tax bracket. He wants to contribute 6 percent of his salary to his 401(k) to meet his company's match. If he chooses a traditional 401(k), his contributions are made with pretax dollars: $2,820 per year (= $47,000 × 0.06), *tax deferred*. He saves that $2,820 from being taxed at 25 percent, so his *yearly tax savings* would be $705 (= $2,820 × 0.25). Adam can pocket that surplus amount for a rainy day or, even better, put it in an IRA to complement his 401(k) for additional retirement income.

Step 2. Estimate your future tax rate and tax bill. We have seen that Adam's 401(k) will grow to $698,248.11 in a traditional account by the time he retires at sixty-seven. The general advice is to withdraw 4 percent each year in retirement, so Adam's "income" amounts to $27,929.92 per year (= $698,248.11 × 0.04).[65] This is less than Adam's current salary and would place him in a lower tax bracket (15 percent). Therefore, his taxes should be lower during retirement than while he was employed (assuming tax rates don't change radically by then).

Step 3. Determine your savings behavior and time horizon to invest. Adam started investing thirteen years later in life than Eve did, and his contribution rate is below the recommended 10–15 percent. For him, I would recommend a traditional 401(k) because his future tax rate will be lower, and he benefits today by saving an extra $705 in a separate account.

Remember: If you choose a traditional account, then save the tax savings! Most millennials might spend the $705, but it's wiser to use it to fund another savings account. If Adam put that amount under his mattress each year until retirement, it would amass to $22,560 (= $705 × 32), but in an IRA that earns 8 percent, it'd grow to $104,737.22 in thirty-two years and give him a total retirement portfolio of $802,985.32 (= $698,248.11 + $104,737.22). With a traditional 401(k) and investment of the tax savings, Adam's portfolio value increases by 15 percent (= $104,737.22/$698,248.11). That's not a bad return.[66]

So for Adam, a traditional 401(k) makes more sense.[67]

A Roth is best for early investors and tax benefits in retirement

Eve, however, started investing promptly at age twenty-two, accumulating $2,287,499.42 by the time she retires at age sixty-seven. She benefits from a forty-five-year time horizon to grow her assets, contributing 7 percent of her annual salary. For her, a Roth 401(k) is a more compelling option. Let's see why.[68]

Step 1. Determine your current tax rate and tax savings. Eve makes the same $47,000 per year that Adam does, so she's also in the current marginal tax bracket of 25 percent. While Adam gets to pocket $705 annually because he contributes pretax dollars to his 401(k), Eve does not get to save $822.50 (= $3,290 × 0.25), because she contributes post-tax dollars on her 7 percent contribution if she chooses a Roth. That is, she pays the taxes on it today—but she will pay no taxes on withdrawals in retirement.

Step 2. Estimate your future tax rate and tax bill. Since Eve started investing at age twenty-two, her 401(k) balance will reach approximately $2,287,499.42 by the time she retires at age sixty-seven. She, too, withdraws only 4 percent of her account each year as her retirement income, or $91,499.98 per year. At that income, she would remain at the 25 percent tax, which is the *same* as her current tax rate. However, assuming she gradually contributes 15 percent to her 401(k) each year, then she'd have even more income in retirement at a *higher* tax rate. Yes, she lives on more in retirement than she did while employed! In other words, her tax liability would be higher, but she doesn't pay a dime of it, since she chose a Roth! (Remember, any employer's matches into a Roth are pretax, but for mathematical simplicity, I gloss over that technicality here.)

Step 3. Determine savings behavior and time horizon to invest. It is true that whereas Eve lost the opportunity to save $822.50 per year while contributing to her Roth 401(k), she gained the ability to forgo paying higher taxes each year in retirement. It is with this compelling case that financial advisors advise that young adults invest in a Roth 401(k). They have time on their side and can save enormously on taxes when they retire.

In sum, for Eve, as well as for any prudent investor starting in his or her twenties, I recommend a Roth 401(k).[69] And for Adam, we have seen that if you've gotten a late start at investing or you want to tax savings today, choose a traditional 401(k).

Still can't decide? Read this!

All right, so maybe I've just thrown a lot of variables at you, and you're a little overloaded. Here's a more distilled version for those who just want a quick-start guide on what to choose:

1. **Choose a traditional 401(k) *if* a Roth 401(k) isn't offered.** In this case, there's no choice and you're stuck with the traditional 401(k). Even if you expect to be in a higher tax bracket at retirement, still invest in the traditional option. You get tax-deferred savings, and the added benefit of an employer's match, if offered.

2. **Choose the Roth 401(k) if you want more certainty about what you will have saved by retirement.** On the other hand, if you want to know exactly what you have earned and don't want to calculate taxes again after retirement, then the Roth is the best option. And, it's the better deal if you start young. (Remember, however, that any employer's matches into a Roth are pretax, and you will pay tax on those withdrawals in retirement.)

3. **Choose a traditional 401(k) if tax savings today incentivizes you to save for retirement in the first place.** No matter what your current or future tax rates are, choose the traditional 401(k) if you want immediate tax savings to spend or, ideally, save. Truthfully, no one knows what tax rates will be in the far-off future. But if the tax savings today incentivize you to start participating in your company's 401(k), according to my recommendations, do it.

4. **Choose both options if you want to hedge your bets about future taxes and add diversification to your retirement investing strategy.** You may have the option to allocate to both account types, though your total contribution can't exceed the annual contribution limit. You could do a fifty-fifty split, allocating, for example, 5 percent to a traditional and 5 percent to a Roth. Knowing that future tax rates are uncertain, this approach adds variety to your 401(k) investing.

When should you do a Roth in-plan conversion?

Let's say you're like Eve—young and saving a lot—and you realize, "Oh, man, I've been investing in a traditional account when I should be investing in a Roth!" Luckily, there is a process called a Roth in-plan conversion. Not all 401(k) plans allow for one, so check with your plan. (**Important note**: No option exists to convert a Roth 401(k) to a traditional 401(k).)

The conversion option could very well help you maximize your retirement savings. You can convert all or a portion. Be careful here, though, because any amounts not taxed previously are taxed as ordinary income in the year of conversion; however, the amount converted to Roth 401(k) and any future investment earnings grow tax-free and will be distributed to you tax-free.

Let's look at an example. Right out of college, you work for four years at a Fortune 500 company. Then, you decide to go back to school for an MBA. You also feel that you should have invested in a Roth 401(k) instead of the traditional account you already have. A sensible tax strategy may be to do your Roth conversion in the year that you are back in school full time. With your tax rate much lower then since you are not working (except perhaps for a summer internship), the tax you'd owe on the conversion would be lower.

Get professional assistance: In this situation, I recommend that you consult with a tax or financial advisor prior to initiating a Roth in-plan conversion to help determine whether this option is right for you. There's a lot to consider here—such as tax-planning strategies, your current and future tax brackets, your current age, and whether you're in a position to pay taxes now on the converted amounts.

Nonprofit and government-employee options: 403(b), 457, TSP

As we have discussed, the 401(k)—either traditional or Roth—is only available through an employer. In addition, it is only private-sector enterprises (i.e., employers that operate to make a profit) that can offer them. What are your alternatives if you work for a nonprofit or the government?

While I will not go through the nuances and minutiae of these non-private-sector accounts, I will provide a quick and easy digest on the options that are structured and operated like a 401(k): the 403(b), the 457, and the TSP. You can get all the details from the IRS.[70]

First, let's look at the 403(b). It is analogous to the 401(k) but geared toward public-school educators and church and nonprofit employees. You can use my recommendations in the exact same way as anyone who has access to a 401(k). You contribute to a 403(b), and your employer may too. Again, you should contribute at least up to any employer's match. Your employer may even authorize a Roth option. Annual contribution limits are the same for the 403(b) and 401(k). All the steps in this book apply to these accounts similarly.

For government employees, there are 457 and Thrift Savings Plan (TSP) retirement plans. Specifically, a 457 is for state and municipal employees (including those who work in public hospitals), and a TSP is for employees of the US government. A 457 or TSP has the same contribution limits as a 401(k) and 403(b), and there may be a Roth option as well.

Important note: 403(b), 457, and TSP plans more commonly than 401(k) plans may offer plan participants the opportunity to invest in fixed and/or variable annuities in addition to mutual-fund options. I would advise you to avoid investing in these products at a younger age. Simply avoid annuities, because they are insurance products and come at a much higher cost, which takes away from your long-term investment returns.

Summary

This chapter was about Step 3 on your way from millennial to millionaire. We went over the two types of 401(k) accounts—traditional and Roth—and how to choose between them. We looked at how their beneficial tax treatments can affect you because of when they apply. While it may be wise to invest in a Roth 401(k) while you are young, you should evaluate four considerations—your current salary, future tax rate, savings behavior, and investing horizon—to decide which account type is better for you. Finally, we discussed non-private-sector retirement-account options such as the 403(b), 457, and TSP.

Step 3 Takeaways

- The two 401(k) accounts, traditional and Roth, each provide preferential tax treatment—but at different times.
- With the traditional, you don't pay taxes on contributions today but on the withdrawals in retirement.
- With the Roth, you pay taxes on contributions today but not on the withdrawals in retirement. Not all employers offer this account.

- The generally accepted financial advice for young adults is to select a Roth, if available in your plan, given their longer investing horizons and the expectation that tax rates will be higher in the future when they retire.
- An investor should consider four key factors when deciding between 401(k) account types: current tax situation, expected future tax rates, savings behavior, and investing time horizon.
- Choose a traditional 401(k) if you want tax savings today.
- Choose a Roth 401(k) if you want no (or minimal, if your employer contributed to the account) taxes in retirement.
- You may have access to a Roth in-plan conversion if your plan allows it. Consult a tax or financial advisor here.
- A 403(b) is the analogue of the 401(k) for public educators, church employees, and nonprofit employees.
- A 457 is for state and local municipal employees, while the Thrift Savings Plan (TSP) is for US government employees.

STEP 4

Design your 401(k) for millionaire success

Enroll in your 401(k) ASAP

At this point, you must be brimming with anticipation to put all this knowledge into practice and be on your way to becoming a millionaire. You have the right mindset and skills sets, how much you need to save while paying down student debt, and how to gradually increase your contribution rate over time. You know how to choose between the Roth and the traditional options. In Step 4, now you are ready to design your 401(k)!

First, open your employer-sponsored 401(k) account! Seems like a no-brainer, right? Well, the truth is that many young adults don't know even where to start, so they procrastinate. Be careful here. Don't end up like Adam and delay opening your 401(k) for over a decade simply because you don't take the time to research your company's enrollment process.

Here's what to do:

1. On the very first day of your first job out of college, find out when you can enroll in your employer-sponsored 401(k).
2. If you can enroll on day one, then do so. Don't put it off. If you must wait a set amount of time (such as a year or so), then set a reminder for yourself this very moment for when you can enroll and then read this list.

If you are already working and haven't yet enrolled but are eligible, then enroll in your 401(k) the first thing after reading this book!

Here's an action item list to enroll in your employer-sponsored 401(k) as soon as possible. (**Important note:** The next steps may be slightly different for every company and the financial institutions they partner with to provide a 401(k), but the essence of the process is the same.)

First, research your plan's enrollment process. Shortly after your hire date, usually the plan provider will send you an enrollment packet. If not, ask your people manager or colleagues about where to find documentation that explains signing up for the 401(k) plan. The enrollment packet probably contains information on when you can start your contributions and how soon after enrollment that any matching contribution will take effect. For example, your company may specify that a new employee can sign up immediately and start making elective contributions but that the matching contribution doesn't begin for one to two pay cycles.

Your company may also inform you of when nonelective contributions will start, if they're offered. They should also have information about when you are fully vested in your earnings. For example, your company may stipulate that you need to be with it for two years to be 100 percent invested (i.e., entitled to all the company's match money. You always own your own contributions and earnings).

Important note: Employers may automatically enroll employees in 401(k) plans at a certain point after hire and at a pretax contribution rate should the employee not make a move to enroll on his or her own. They may also place the contribution automatically in a target-date retirement fund aligned to your anticipated retirement date. If you want to contribute a different amount than from the automatic enrollment, make Roth contributions and make investment elections, then make sure to update your preferences.

Second, register at the plan provider's website. Your enrollment packet should contain information about the plan provider. You'll go through the usual kind of online registration process but won't need to provide any bank account information. Your contributions will be sent to the plan provider directly out of your gross pay. Remember to name a beneficiary for your account. Your beneficiary will be able to inherit your account balance in the unfortunate event of your death.

Third, choose your contribution rate. Specify a contribution that's at least up to the employer's match if you can't begin at 10–15 percent of your salary (refer to Step 2).

Fourth, select a Roth or traditional account. Not all companies offer the Roth option, but if yours does, remember the recommendations. The Roth is usually best for young investors and those who want tax savings in retirement, and the traditional is for late starters and those who want to benefit from tax savings today (refer to Step 3).

Important note: Once enrolled, many folks unfortunately stop here. But you still need to define your investing profile and select funds to contribute to. The next step is to select the investments that you want to invest in to make money!

Be an "aggressive investor" to accumulate millions

The next step in designing your 401(k) plan for millionaire success is to choose the correct investing profile, which you need to do before even starting to invest in your 401(k). As a DIY investor, you'll need to define this for yourself, but it's straightforward to do. It is a representation of the characteristics that make you the kind of investor that you are. Your investing profile is your blueprint for how to invest your 401(k) money, and there are three general types of investing profile:

1. **Aggressive.** This profile emphasizes capital appreciation as the primary investment objective—you want your money to grow exponentially. You attempt to maximize return with a higher degree of risk. More emphasis is placed on investing in stocks compared to bonds or short-term reserves. The investing time horizon here is long term (fifteen-to-forty-plus years).
2. **Balanced.** This profile aims to balance risk and reward. Often the weighting is equally split between stock and bonds. The profile focuses on capital preservation as the primary investment objective—you want to keep your money stable. The investing time horizon is between ten and fifteen years.

3. **Fixed-income.** This profile stresses capital preservation with a guaranteed income stream—you want to keep your money static and live off of its earnings in retirement. You get less reward for much less risk. The profile invests in bonds compared to stocks. You want to live off the proceeds here for as long as your retirement (fifteen to twenty years—up to thirty years).

For reference, the category an investor fits in is based on your answers to the investing goals (how much wealth you want to achieve), time horizon (how much time you have to invest), and risk tolerance (how much fluctuation you are willing to tolerate in the market) you have. As a young investor and millennial, the best category for you is an aggressive profile. You have more than thirty to forty years to achieve the income that you need for a secure retirement. For the best results, your investments should ideally be 100 percent (or at least 90 percent) in stocks (versus bonds or other asset classes).

Each investing profile implies the pursuit of a certain blend of three primary asset classes. These are stocks, bonds, and short-term reserves. Let's consider each of them.

Stocks

A stock is a piece (i.e., a share) of ownership in a business venture. Ideally, investment returns on a stock provide (but do not guarantee!) price appreciation. Some also offer dividend returns. Dividends are periodic payments from stock investments because you've given your money for a company to use in its business operations. A company can choose a quarterly, biannual, or annual schedule. Your mutual funds receive these from the companies in your funds, and they go into your account. Dividend payments are one of the two ways that you make money by investing in stocks (the other is when you sell a stock for a higher price that you paid for it, after owning it over the long term).

So what does all this mean? When you purchase a share or shares in a company, you are technically an owner of the company and therefore entitled to that portion of its earnings and assets. The company you invest in wants its earnings to grow so that you, as an investor, will continue to invest in it. How does the company you invest in use your money? It may conduct research and development, expand operations, and launch new products and services.

Stocks are classified into three categories based on market capitalization ("market cap"), which is a company's stock price multiplied by the total number of shares it offers in the market. Each category has different potential for reward and risk:

- **Large-cap** companies have a market cap over $5 billion. They are more established companies, most likely those on the S&P 500, that might offer slower capital appreciation but are more generous with consistent dividend income over time. Large-cap stocks are more stable and pose less risk to investors than mid- and small-cap stocks.
- **Mid-cap** companies have a market cap between $1 billion and $5 billion. These companies are growing and offer higher appreciation on the value of their shares and sometimes offer dividend income. Mid-cap stocks are on a path to stability but can offer higher returns—and higher risk—to investors.
- **Small-cap** companies have a market cap less than $1 billion. They are newer to the market and have a lot of upswing potential in terms of capital (share price) appreciation. Given their higher growth projections, they may not offer dividends. These stocks carry the most volatility (price fluctuation) but offer the highest return potential compared to large-cap and mid-cap stocks.

Bonds

A bond is an asset class that represents you giving a loan to a business or the government. Bond investment returns come in the form of guaranteed income payments; they have lower price appreciation than stocks. So what does this mean? When you purchase a company's or the government's bond, you are a creditor to them, and therefore they are required to pay back what you loaned them, called the principal, plus interest— which is what they pay you for borrowing your money (just like you pay interest on a car loan or credit card). A company may use your loaned money the same way as one whose stock you hold (i.e., for research and development, etc.).

Short-Term Reserves

Short-term reserves are basically cash and cash equivalents—such as checking accounts, savings accounts, and certificates of deposit. So what does this mean? Instead of giving money to a company or the government, you put it in a checking or savings accounts at a bank, and they can loan out your money to other clients. The bank provides interest on the money that you place with them, but it is usually very low (less than 1 percent). How does a bank use your money? They may make auto loans and mortgages to other customers.

To get the highest growth possible, you should mostly or completely invest your money in stock investments. I've given you the numbers on how to transform yourself from a millennial into a millionaire if certain conditions are met. To achieve your retirement goals, you should contribute as much as you can (10–15 percent) for as long as you can (forty-five-plus years) in stocks.

Recommendation: Choose an aggressive profile in your twenties and thirties to accrue the powerful benefits of time and compounding found in stock exposure.

Three ingredients to build your investment portfolio

In Step 2, you saw how much you needed to save in your 401(k) to get into the millions. To align those goals to an aggressive investor profile, it's now time to build your investment portfolio. The three ingredients for doing this are as follows:

1. **Asset allocation**
2. **Diversification**
3. **Selecting funds to minimize costs**

If you construct your 401(k) portfolio according to these three principles, you'll have a well-diversified and low-cost portfolio that can set you up on course more likely toward millionaire success by retirement. But again, even though the stock market produces 8 percent over the long term, remember that past performance is not a guarantee of future returns. Let's take a look into each ingredient.

Allocate your assets toward stock

Without question, asset allocation is by far the most important ingredient into achieving your wealth goals.[71] Asset allocation is dividing your investments among a mixture of the asset classes (i.e., stocks, bonds, and short-term reserves). You allocate based on your investment goals, investing time horizon, and risk tolerance. As an aggressive investor, your asset allocation will be mostly (or all) in stock, because that gives you the highest expected return possible over the long term.

Many factors affect how your 401(k) portfolio grows over the long term. Fluctuations in the stock market (e.g., as influenced by geopolitical strife like contentious political elections or terrorism) will make your portfolio go up and down over the short term. In the medium term, economic recession and expansion and the ups and downs of business cycles impact how your portfolio performs. You could hedge against these fluctuations with a mixture of stocks and bonds, because, as a general rule, when stocks go up, bonds go down, and vice versa. But when you are young and time is on your side, you can weather these temporary market downturns. The best advice is to stay calm and assured that your portfolio will bounce back.

When you are young, you want to take calculated risks, because higher returns come with higher risks. You don't want to play it too safe and invest mainly in safer assets like bonds or cash, because with those, the returns tend to be much lower over time. However, research from the Transamerica Center for Retirement Studies shows only 21 percent of millennials are invested mostly in stocks, and 32 percent are invested in an equal mix of stocks and bonds.[72] With so many years ahead of you, this trend is disconcerting. To maximize growth, you want to be invested

100 percent (or no less than 90 percent) in the stock market when you are a young investor.

Let's look at an example to illustrate the power of asset allocation toward stock compared to bonds over a long-term horizon. Stocks have averaged 8 percent over the long term, while bonds historically have averaged 5 percent. Let's go back to our pal Eve, who invested 7 percent of her income starting at age twenty-two (see DIY 401(k) Math, Case 1). How would 100 percent invested in stocks compared to 100 percent invested in bonds impact the growth of Eve's 401(k) balance over ten to fifty years?[73]

	100% stocks	100% bonds
10 years		
	$79,024.04	$66,995.94
20 years		
	$254,679.38	$177,400.56
30 years		
	$645,127.69	$359,339.61
40 years		
	$1,513,019.72	$659,162.40
50 years		
	$3,442,178.02	$1,153,249.33

Figure 10: 401(k) balance in 100 percent stocks versus
100 percent bonds over ten to fifty years

What we observe here is that a 100 percent stock asset allocation grows much faster over time, providing much more retirement income. A 100 percent bond allocation limits the ability of your 401(k) account to reach its full growth potential. The difference is slighter after twenty years, but after forty or fifty years, it is more substantial.

Recommendation: Go for a 100 percent stock asset allocation to get the highest investment return over the long term. You have thirty or forty years to recoup from any market downturns. If 100 percent stock makes you too uneasy, then you can scale back some on the stock exposure but still with no less than 90 percent of your 401(k) in the stock market. This allocation gets you as much capital appreciation as possible.

Diversify your allocation among domestic and international stock
After you have allocated your assets among the asset classes, there's a more granular level of asset allocation called "diversification." It can add to your growth potential. Asset allocation is concerned with the proportion of stocks, bonds, and cash; diversification zeroes in on how to allocate your money *within* an asset class according to industry sector, market capitalization, and geography. For example, within the stock and bond asset classes, we can decide to invest specifically in the following:

- Domestic stock
  o Large-cap
  o Mid-cap
  o Small-cap
- International stock
  o Developed countries
  o Emerging economies
- Bonds
  o Government
  o Commercial

For diversification, within the stock asset class, it's considered ideal to have a mixture of US and international equity exposures to hedge risk. Within domestic stock, there is a further level of diversification between what is known as growth and value stocks. Within each market capitalization, you could select a combination of either categories. Growth stocks are expected to experience faster-than-expected growth, whereas value stocks are undervalued in the market but still worth the investment.[74]

Recommendation: To optimize your 401(k) for millionaire success with the best possible diversification, I recommend a portfolio with the following asset allocation and diversification, focused exclusively on exposure to domestic and international stock:

- Seventy percent domestic stock
  - Forty percent large-cap
  - Fifteen percent mid-cap
  - Fifteen percent small-cap
- Thirty percent international stock
  - Twenty-five percent developed countries
  - Five percent emerging economies

Select the low-cost investments your plan offers

Let's take a deeper dive into the common investment options you *might* see in your 401(k) plan. Remember, your plan sponsor will have a predetermined list of investment funds, and while each 401(k) plan is different, generally, you may see a sampling of actively managed mutual funds, index mutual funds, target-date retirement funds, and company stock (if you work for a publicly traded firm). In any case, selecting the investment funds that minimize investing costs will increase your investment returns because you get to keep more of your money over the long term.

Mutual Funds

A mutual fund is a vehicle for investing in a pool of asset classes, such as a bundle of domestic stocks or corporate bonds. One benefit of a mutual fund is the instant diversification you get at once instead of having to invest in hundreds of single stocks. A downside, though, is that each mutual fund comes with an expense ratio (cost of the fund expressed as a percentage of the fund's total assets). A lot of mutual funds are "actively managed," meaning that there is an investment manager behind the scenes who picks and chooses which assets the fund adds and subtracts. These funds have higher expense ratios.

Index Funds

Index funds are mutual funds whose holdings mirror the collection of stocks that make up an index. An index tracks the value of a portfolio of stocks that are considered to reflect trends in the broader stock market in some way. These funds are considered "passively managed" because indexes don't have someone actively adding and subtracting stocks—they hold the stocks that are in the index. Index funds give investors access to broad market exposure at a minimal cost since they track the market instead of trying to outperform it like actively managed funds do. Their lower expense ratios may consequently contribute to higher long-term investor returns.[75]

Two important stock indexes to be familiar with that index funds may track are as follows:

- **The Dow Jones Industrial Average (DJIA).** This is the oldest index. It contains thirty of the largest and most prestigious companies in the United States, including Apple, General Electric, and McDonald's. When people in the financial world refer to "the stock market," they mean this index.
- **Standard & Poor's 500 (S&P 500).** This index includes five hundred of the most widely held companies, offering exceptional diversification exposure and capturing 70 percent of the overall US stock market.

Target-Date Retirement Funds

Target-date retirement funds, also known as lifecycle funds, are mutual funds that automatically reset the asset allocation in its portfolio according to a maturity date, which in this case is the retirement horizon. These funds offer instant diversification into the stock market although expense ratios for them can vary. Any target date that you see must have a target date of 2050/2060, which is the time period when millennials are expected to retire, and with that maturity date the fund will be more heavily exposed to stock compared to bonds. As you get closer to retirement, your target-date fund focuses less on stock and more on bonds.

How to Select Mutual Funds to Maximize Return and Minimize Cost

Now you know what the difference is between actively managed funds, index mutual funds, and target-date retirement funds. How can you decide which funds have the best potential to help you achieve your retirement investing goals? Out of these three investment options, I recommend that you select the mutual funds in your 401(k) that meet the following two requirements:

1. **Demonstrates a proven track record of high returns.** The fund should have a reasonably high ten-year investment return or Life of Fund return, which is the investment return since the fund's inception. Either should be greater than or equal to 8 percent, which is the long-term stock market average return.

2. **Shows the fund is committed to keeping expense ratios low.** The fund should have a reasonably low expense ratio (around 0.50 percent, if actively managed). But strive to go even lower with index mutual funds, *if* available. The average expense ratio for an index fund is less than 0.25 percent.[76]

Take time to peruse the investment options your 401(k) plan offers, and do analysis on which of the mutual funds meet these two criteria: give you highest long-term investment returns and provide the lowest expense ratios. Don't cherry pick funds, but be methodical and analytical here to ensure you are picking the best funds for your investing goals.

What fees do you pay in your 401(k)?

As a DIY investor, which you will certainly become after reading this book, you will have the aptitude to manage your 401(k) yourself with confidence. You, yourself, will possess the credentials to assume the role of boss of your 401(k)'s upkeep and destiny. This management is zero cost to you, except for the time and effort you put into learning about investing and managing your 401(k) account. It will start to feel more like a fulfilling pastime than tedious work. Since you are going to self-manage, let's get acclimated to the fees that you will most likely encounter in your plan and talk about strategies on how to reduce these fees so that you are left with higher investment returns.

401(k) fees

To begin with, and to recall, your employer will partner with a plan provider, such as Fidelity or Morgan Stanley, etc. to provide you the 401(k) plan and run the day-to-day activities of your plan. For example, you will enroll in your 401(k) with the plan provider, and it is with them that you will select your contribution rate and which investment funds to contribute to. Smaller and midsized companies may also have a separate plan advisor in addition to the plan provider. The plan advisor may help with enrollment and/or manage your 401(k), for a fee. Larger plans may provide access to portfolio advisory services, where you get a team of investment professionals behind the scenes who help design and manage your 401(k), for a fee too.

Knowing that your 401(k) plan is managed by a third party, naturally there are costs associated with this work. These costs can be grouped mainly into the three main categories of 401(k) fees:

1. **Expense ratios.** As mentioned, this is the cost of the investment funds you select in your plan for overall operating expenses, expressed as a percentage of the fund's total assets.
2. **Advisory fees.** These are the fees you'd pay if you elect to hire the plan advisor or portfolio advisory services to manage and adjust your 401(k) investment portfolio for you. This fee can be higher than 0.50 percent of your account value on top of the expense ratios you pay for each investment.
3. **Administrative fees.** These are fees paid to the plan provider for recordkeeping, compliance, communication with participants, and transactions processing.

There are other costs, but these are the main three general expenses. Costs are lower for the largest plans, such as those provided by publically traded companies, think like Goldman Sachs and Apple, where the company can negotiate lower fees and access to cheaper classes of fund, such as index funds, with the plan provider. Smaller and midsized companies typically have more expensive plans because there is less scale to distribute the costs among its participants. Employers generally will not cover these administrative fees and pass them onto plan participants.

How can you lower your 401(k) costs?

As an investor, you can't control market returns. (Although recall that the long-term stock market return is 8 percent.) But you can contain the costs that you pay in your 401(k). When you minimize your investing costs, you can get a higher overall investment return. For each of the three 401(k) expenses, here's how you can minimize expenses:

1. **Expense ratio.** Choose low-cost index funds over actively managed funds, if available in your 401(k) plan. If index funds aren't available, then select the lowest-cost actively managed funds.
2. **Advisory fee.** Select to DIY your 401(k)! Don't elect to have a plan advisor or portfolio advisory services design and manage your 401(k). You can avoid professional investment management fees by following the steps enumerated in this book!
3. **Administrative fee.** Unfortunately, you have zero control over this, and you will have to pay what is charged to you. This fee will be deducted from your account balance.

So, in sum, select low-cost index funds (if your plan offers them), and avoid the plan advisor/portfolio advisory services to lower your overall investing expenses.[77]

The Fiduciary Rule in one paragraph

Maybe you have heard of the Fiduciary Rule, but you aren't too sure what it is. First off, "fiduciary" means having *trust* between you and a financial professional. The Department of Labor implemented the Fiduciary Rule on June 9, 2017. The rule essentially looks to limit potential conflicts of interest between you and plan advisors. If your plan has a plan advisor, he or she will need to act more in your best interest instead of promoting products in the plan that best suit them but recommend products aligned to your retirement goals, risk tolerance, and investing time horizon. Additionally, the rule also means that 401(k) fees will need to be more transparent and communicated to you.[78]

How to design your millionaire 401(k) portfolio today

Now it's time to construct your 401(k) portfolio using the three ingredients I've just discussed to maximize return and minimize cost to you over the long term. Keep in mind that your employer will select both the plan provider, which could be any one of many financial services companies, as well as the investment funds in your plan, which may or may not include target-date retirement funds and/or index funds.

When it comes to 401(k) portfolio construction, a benefit is you choose the investment funds available while a drawback is its set of limited options for low-cost investing. In fact, any given plan may provide at most only one index mutual fund, which is likely to be large-cap oriented—such as an S&P 500 index fund. Yet most plans offer at least three investment funds, while the average plan offers eight to twelve options.

Here I present three hypothetical 401(k) portfolios you can construct to achieve a millionaire's retirement. This presentation of portfolio construction is intended for general illustration. Any specific financial services companies and investment funds mentioned here are used solely for illustrative purposes. As discussed, whatever your specific plan offers, make sure to select funds that have high long-term returns and the lowest expense ratios to construct and optimize your 401(k) portfolio.

The Target-Date Retirement Fund Portfolio

Not too sure what to invest in yet? Then invest in a target-date retirement fund to get your feet wet with DIY investing. As a quick start to just get into the stock market as soon as you possibly can without selecting individual funds, you may choose to invest in a target-date retirement fund, *if* your plan offers it. Make sure to select a target-date retirement fund aligned to your expected retirement time frame—around 2050 or 2060—because that will give you the most stock market exposure. These funds give you immediate diversification. Note that expense ratios do differ. As you evolve your DIY strength, move on to the next portfolio to build a low-cost index-fund portfolio.

The Index Funds-Only Portfolio

When you are confident and comfortable with your DIY skills, then move on to construct a portfolio of low-cost index funds. Let's say that it takes you a year or so to feel confident to construct your portfolio as a DIY investor. As a next step, you can exchange the target-date retirement fund for a portfolio of low-cost index funds that you choose on your own, *if* your plan offers them. This is the ideal portfolio. For illustrative purposes, here's an example of what this portfolio might look like in this type of situation[79]:

- For 70 percent domestic-stock exposure:
  - Fidelity 500 Index Fund (40 percent)
  - Fidelity Mid-Cap Index Fund (15 percent)
  - Fidelity Small-Cap Index Fund (15 percent)
- For 30 percent international-stock exposure
  - Fidelity International Index Fund (25 percent)
  - Fidelity Emerging Markets Index Fund (5 percent)

The Hybrid Index Funds and Lowest-Cost Actively Managed Funds Portfolio

If your plan doesn't offer this many index funds or none at all, substitute the lowest-cost actively managed funds where appropriate. You may have a 401(k) plan that offers index funds for all stock asset subclasses, or they may offer index funds for some subclasses, or even none at all, giving you no choice but to invest in actively managed funds. In which case, select the lowest-cost actively mutual funds. Additionally, your plan may offer you a mixture of funds from other financial institutions as well. For instance, you may see index and actively managed mutual funds from a mix of firms such as Vanguard, T. Rowe Price, Charles Schwab, just to name a few. For illustrative purposes, here's an example of what this portfolio might look like in this type of situation:

- For 70 percent domestic-stock exposure:
    o Fidelity 500 Index Fund (40 percent)
    o Hartford Mid-Cap Fund (15 percent)
    o Russell 250 Index Fund (15 percent)
- For 30 percent international-stock exposure
    o Vanguard Total World Stock Index Fund (25 percent)
    o Lazard Emerging Markets Equity Portfolio (5 percent)

Notice that the mid-cap mutual fund, Hartford Mid-Cap Fund, and the emerging markets mutual fund, Lazard Emerging Markets Equity Portfolio, are not index funds but actively managed funds. You may have no choice here if these are the only options for these asset subclasses. This is not the ideal portfolio, but it is an acceptable portfolio.

Investments to avoid in your twenties and thirties
Avoid the following investment funds in twenties and thirties, if offered in your 401(k) plan:

1. **Variable annuities**. This is a hybrid insurance product, combining funds that resemble mutual funds with insurance protection guaranteeing that your plan beneficiary will get back your principal if you die before taking out withdrawals. While you would get stock exposure here, these funds have higher management fees than mutual funds, and additionally while annuities may be sensible products for older investors who need guaranteed income for themselves and beneficiaries, you have time to grow and preserve your 401(k) with (index) mutual funds.[80]
2. **Stable value funds**. These funds guarantee the value of your contributions on top of a fixed rate of return. They invest in

government and corporate bonds. These funds don't provide the exposure you need to stock early on.[81]

3. **Guaranteed investment contracts (GICs).** GICs are insurance products that resemble individual bonds. You don't get the exposure you must have to stock and additionally the issuer uses your money for the term of the contract at a fixed rate of return.[82]

4. **Target-date retirement funds that mature before 2050/2060.** Target-date retirement funds are fine, if the maturity date aligns to your expected retirement horizon. For a millennial, if it is less than 2050/2060, then your portfolio will be overexposed to bonds, shortchanging you the opportunity to earn higher returns.

Recommendation: To get into the stock market quickly and build your DIY skills, start with a target-date retirement fund aligned to your expected retirement time frame—around 2050 or 2060. As you grow in your DIY investing journey, build a portfolio of low-cost index mutual funds. If you must, round out your portfolio with the lowest-cost actively managed mutual funds that have the highest long-term returns.

Three tips to boost your returns

This next section is more intermediate level investing. I cannot stress enough that the most important element in your long-term success is your asset allocation. In your case as a millennial who has thirty or forty years until retirement, your asset allocation should be exclusively in (index) mutual funds invested in stocks. To add an extra bump to your earning potential that you can sow in your early investing years, here are three tips that I've used to put myself on a faster-than-average course to millions.

Mid-cap mutual funds are the "sweet spot"

Over the past couple of years, mid-cap funds have provided high returns with not that much risk relative to typically riskier investments like small-cap funds. In fact, a lot of research has called mid-caps the "sweet spot" of investing.[83] A leading mid-cap index, the S&P MidCap 400, has returned 9 percent over the past ten years. Mid-cap companies have demonstrated proven track records of delivering shareholder value, but they have more room to expand too. Mid-cap funds give you a combination of firms that demonstrate relative organizational stability but with the agility to adapt to the market with higher speed than large-cap corporations. The asset-allocation and diversification model that I presented above calls for 15 percent of your portfolio to be in mid-cap, but if you're willing to take more calculated risk and earn more reward, there's potential benefit in allocating more of your holdings (~25 percent) to mid-cap mutual funds.

Take advantage of the "small-cap premium"

You can also earn higher returns by investing in small-cap mutual funds. Standard asset allocation and diversification calls for 15 percent in small-caps, but if you are willing to take on more calculated risk in the long term, you can significantly benefit from allocating more (roughly 20 percent) to small-cap funds. You can usually get small-cap funds at a bargain price compared to what the market expects the company to be earning well into the future, meaning a higher investment return. So if you invest in small-cap mutual funds, your return could be higher than if you invested everything in the S&P 500, which consists exclusively of large-cap companies. US small-cap stocks have returned 12 percent over the long term, while the S&P 500 from 1950 to 2016 has returned 8 percent. When you are young, you should consider investing in small-caps.

Select to reinvest your company stock dividends

When it comes to how you like to receive your dividends from your 401(k) plan, if you invest in mutual funds, any dividends received are *automatically* reinvested into more shares of the same fund. However, if you select to invest in your company's stock, if offered in your plan, then you will have the option to choose on how you want to receive those dividends. Remember, and for the record, I don't recommend that you buy your employer's stock but instead that you maximize returns and minimize your costs with a diversified portfolio of low-cost (preferably, index) mutual funds.

When it comes to stock dividends, you will have two election options. First, you can receive them as a cash distribution. What happens here is that the dividend will be paid to you as a cash distribution. The dividend you receive is taxable income. Second, you can reinvest it back into the company stock. What happens here is the dividends you receive will be reinvested automatically back into the stock and will be used to purchase additional shares. The reinvested dividend is not taxable income. If you choose to invest a proportion of your contributions into your company's stock, then most definitely select to reinvest the dividends to avoid taxes and to accelerate 401(k) account growth.[84]

Summary

This chapter was about designing your 401(k)'s portfolio of investments. Now you have all the knowledge you need to design your account. You know the critical importance of opening an employer-sponsored 401(k) as soon as you are eligible, and we walked through the general enrollment process. We discussed the three general types of investing profiles—aggressive, balanced, and fixed-income—and there is a compelling case for why you should be an aggressive investor in your twenties and thirties. You may start your 401(k) portfolio with a target-date retirement fund and then move on to index funds or to low-cost actively managed funds if index funds aren't available. And I advised on funds not to invest in that your plan may offer. Last, I gave you three ways to add an extra boost to your 401(k) earnings while you are young.

Step 4 Takeaways

- Open a 401(k) with your employer as soon as you're eligible.
- Choose an aggressive investing profile in your twenties and thirties.
- Ideally invest 100 percent in the stock market, but no less than at least 90 percent of your account in stocks in your twenties and thirties.

- Diversify among asset subclasses, such as domestic and international stock, with the following asset allocation mix:
  1. Seventy percent domestic stock
     - Forty percent large-cap
     - Fifteen percent mid-cap
     - Fifteen percent small-cap
  2. Thirty percent international stock
     - Twenty-five percent developed countries
     - Five percent emerging countries
- Use these three tips to reduce your 401(k) fees and investing costs:
  1. Choose (index) mutual funds with the lowest expense ratios.
  2. Avoid the advisory fees and instead DIY your portfolio.
  3. You can't change or control the administrative fees.
- Depending on what investment options your 401(k) plan offers, here's three portfolios to you could construct:
  1. To get into the market, start with a target-date retirement fund (one that matures in your retirement year) to get instant diversification.
  2. Next, build a portfolio with low-cost index mutual funds, if available.
  3. If (some or all) index mutual funds are not available to cover all your asset allocations, then select the lowest-cost actively managed funds.
- Do not invest in
  1. variable annuities,
  2. stable value funds,
  3. guaranteed investment contracts (GICs), or
  4. target-date retirement funds that mature before 2050/2060.
- Three tips on how to get an extra boost to your long-term earnings are as follows:
  1. Invest 25 percent in mid-cap funds.
  2. Invest 20 percent in small-cap funds.
  3. Select to reinvest the dividends of stock in your employing company.

STEP 5

Manage your 401(k) for continued success

Rebalance to keep your portfolio fit

I n Step 5, after you set up your 401(k) account through the plan provider your employer has partnered with and after you have designed your 401(k) portfolio for millionaire success, it's time to do a little review. To begin, you want to know your year-to-date (YTD) investment return and your current versus target asset allocation.

As for the first item, at your plan provider's website, your account typically reports your YTD investment return. You will also most likely receive quarterly and an annual statement that will show your investment return. It is very important to note that you should not panic if this number is negligible or even negative! Your account will certainly be subject to short-term fluctuations in the stock market, but remember that you're investing for the long term. Over a longer period, your account is likely to deliver positive returns; the stock market has averaged around an 8 percent investment return.

As for the second item, you will assess your current versus target asset allocation, and if you're off target, you'll do some rebalancing. As the stock market goes up or down, the amount of your holdings allocated to each of your chosen asset subclasses changes. So, over time, your allocation may move out of alignment with your target allocation. Essentially, "rebalancing" is getting your account's current asset allocation back to its target asset allocation. I advise rebalancing once a year at the maximum and no more than that per year.

As I've noted, your investing profile guides you to choose a pre-defined asset-allocation mix of stocks, bonds, and cash. As an aggressive investor, your asset allocation should be ideally 100 percent stock only, or at least 90 percent stocks and 10 percent bonds. When you first invest, this current asset allocation is, of course, aligned exactly with your target asset allocation. But as time progresses, they diverge.

To demonstrate rebalancing, let's return to our friend Eve. She's now invested for twelve years, accumulating about $100,000 in her 401(k), and her asset allocation is 90 percent stock (invested in a stock mutual fund) and 10 percent bonds (invested in a bond mutual fund). (To check the math, go to Case 9 in "DIY 401(k) Math" and replicate those steps, inputting 12 into *nper* in your Excel formula.) By the end of the year, the stock market has risen 8 percent, and the bond market has dropped 5 percent. At that point, what is the portfolio's asset allocation? And if it's not equal to the target allocation (90/10), what must be done?

Because the stock market rose and the bond market dropped, the value of the stock mutual fund in the 401(k) account rose to 91 percent of its overall value while the value of its bond mutual fund dropped to 9 percent of it. Your new account value is $106,700 (= ($90,000 × 1.08) + ($10,000 × 0.95)). So the account is considered overweighed in stocks by 1 percent and underweighted in bonds by 1 percent.

What does the account holder do to rebalance it to its target allocation mix? Rebalancing is the act of selling items that appreciated and buying items that depreciated. So here, you would sell the stock mutual fund to get back to 90 percent and buy the bond mutual fund to get back up to 10 percent. It's as straightforward as that. What does this look like in practice?

1. **Sell the assets that have appreciated.** At the end of the year, the account balance is $106,700, and you now have $97,200 in stock (= $90,000 × 1.08), which gives you 91 percent stock exposure (= $97,200/$106,700). But you want 90 percent stock exposure, which amounts to $96,030 (= 0.9 × $106,700). To rebalance, you sell the difference, which is $1,170 (= $97,200 − $96,030).

2. **Buy the assets that have depreciated.** Similarly, your $10,000 in bonds dropped to $9,500 (= $10,000 × 0.95), giving you 9 percent bond exposure (= $9,500/$106,700). But you want 10 percent bond exposure, which amounts to $10,670 (= 0.1 × $106,700). To rebalance, you buy the difference, which is also $1,170 (= $10,670 – $9,500).

To rebalance your account, you can change your current investment funds by executing an exchange. To get the investment mix that you want (for instance, to rebalance your portfolio), you can swap one investment for another, or you can exchange multiple investments. When you execute an exchange, you simultaneously sell a current holding in a mutual fund and buy a new one. For example, let's say you currently divide your investing between Mutual Funds A and B but now want to switch everything into Mutual Funds C and D. Once you do this exchange, you no longer own Mutual Funds A or B, and all the money held in those funds will transfer to Mutual Funds C and D.

Recommendation: Rebalance your 401(k) account no more than once a year. Rebalancing is only for aligning your current asset allocation with your target asset allocation to meet your personalized retirement goals. To this end, you may change your current allocations through making an exchange.

Of note, you can also change your contribution allocations going forward, which is different from an exchange. Let's say that you have been splitting your contributions 50 percent between Mutual Funds A and B. In the future, you want instead 50 percent to go each to Mutual Fund C and to Mutual Fund D. For example, unlike an exchange where you buy and sell mutual funds, you will still own Mutual Funds A and B (and the existing money stays there), but going forward your contributions will go only to Mutual Funds C and D. You can do this if you want to keep money in a fund but no longer contribute to, instead redirecting your money into new funds for added diversification.

Digital options for managing your wealth

Take advantage of today's digital wealth-management platforms that allow you to combine all your accounts for a comprehensive picture of your entire financial portfolio, including your checking, savings, credit-card, and mortgage accounts. The top two tools that I recommend are these:

- Personal Capital
- Mint.com

In fact, 80 percent of millennials indicate that they would prefer to use mobile apps to self-manage their 401(k)s.[85] These sites are free, and their mobile apps give a holistic view of all your assets (cash, retirement accounts) and liabilities (credit card, student debt). These two items calculate your net worth (= assets − liabilities). The apps also provide tools for budgeting and setting financial goals.

Personal Capital also provides analytical tools such as a retirement planner and 401(k) fee analyzer. With these, you can see if you are on track to reach your retirement goals and assess whether you are paying too much for mutual funds in your 401(k) plan. They can recommend corrective action if you should need to take any.

Avoid these common 401(k) mistakes!

Millennials tend to make certain common mistakes when managing 401(k)s on their own. They derail your ability to benefit from the power of compound interest and maximize your investments in the long term. Here are the six most common mistakes to avoid:

- **Leaving your company before you are fully vested in your 401(k).** We've gone over the fact that when you leave your employer, you are not entitled to its matching contributions (and its earnings) unless you are vested. Conduct due diligence on your company's vesting process and know what you are giving up if you are not vested.
- **Taking a loan from your 401(k).** Around 87 percent of 401(k) plans allow employees to borrow from their plans through a loan. In addition, you may think you'll only take a loan once, but the problem is that once you borrow from your 401(k), research shows that you're likely to do it again.[86] If you don't pay the loan back, it is treated like an early withdrawal, with applicable

penalties and taxes. Instead, save in an emergency fund to pay for life's unexpected expenses so you don't impede retirement savings. (Not sure how to budget for an emergency fund? Go back to Step 2 and check out "How to budget like a millionaire.")

- **Withdrawing from your 401(k) before age fifty-nine and a half.** Your 401(k) is an investment vehicle in which to save for retirement, and the IRS stipulates that funds are not to be withdrawn until the account holder is fifty-nine and a half or incur a 10 percent tax penalty, bar certain exemptions. Just don't do it!

- **Investing your entire portfolio in your company's stock.** As I've noted, I recommend that you diversify your assets by allocating them into low-cost (index) mutual funds and not buy your employer's own stock. Investing all your portfolio into one stock is highly risky (no matter which stock it might be), because your gains and losses are those of only one company. It may seem safe to put all your money in your company's stock, but it isn't.

- **Rebalancing your 401(k) account too frequently.** Rebalance no more than once per year to maintain your target asset allocation. Avoid knee-jerk reactions when the market goes high or low in the short term. Don't sell or buy according to your convenience, either. Set a proper yearly rebalancing schedule and stick to it.

- **Reducing your contribution rate to finance big purchases.** You may feel the urge to reduce your contribution rate or stop contributing all together when you anticipate big expenses such as a house, a new car, or a child. Understandably, these are expensive situations, but you need to keep investing toward your retirement. Find alternative ways to finance life's big purchases, such as through more disciplined budgeting and building up an emergency savings fund. (Not sure how to budget or even how to budget for an emergency fund? Go back to Step 2 and check out "How to budget like a millionaire.")

When to do a 401(k) rollover

The last part of managing a 401(k) is the 401(k) rollover. When you leave the company that has held your account, you have three options for your money:

- **Keep your 401(k) in your former employer's plan if it allows that.** However, even if offered, your former employer may not allow you to keep your money in its 401(k) plan if the balance is less than $5,000 anyway. This option may be beneficial if, let's say, you switch from a direct hire role that offered a 401(k) to a contract role that doesn't offer a 401(k) but you expect to move back into a direct hire role soon that offers a 401(k) again. In that case, keeping your plan in your former employer's plan during this work transition period may make the most sense. Your savings keep their tax-favored growth potential, and you can typically keep your current investments but additional contributions will not be allowed.
- **Roll over your 401(k) into your new employer's 401(k) plan.** You may be able to roll over your money to your new employer, but check with them first. One advantage to this option is that you can continue to make additional contributions (up to the annual limit) right on top of your existing balance that you roll over. Of course, you'll also want to check to see if your new employer's 401(k) plan offers attractive and low-cost investment options. It might or might not.
- **Roll over your 401(k) into a rollover IRA.** This option is popular, because an IRA gives you access to a wider selection of lower-cost investment options, particularly index mutual funds, than a 401(k) typically offers. And, if you have a Roth 401(k), you can roll it over into a Roth IRA. Unlike the Roth 401(k), there are no required minimum distributions for a Roth IRA after age seventy and a half, so you may keep your money growing tax-free for the rest of your life. You can even leave all or a portion of the Roth IRA upon death to your beneficiaries, which they can enjoy tax-free, too! A downside, however, is your annual contribution is less than a 401(k)'s.

Get professional assistance: Before you do a rollover, I recommend that you consult with a tax or financial advisor to see which option is best for your financial situation. Do *not*, under any circumstance, cash out your 401(k) when you change jobs! Your early withdrawals may be subject to a 10 percent penalty fee if under age fifty-nine and a half, along with any applicable ordinary income taxes, and you lose out on retirement savings and future tax-favored potential growth.

Congratulate yourself on your success

You've come to the end of this book, the premier guide for the digital generation making its way in the world of personal finance, retirement planning, and investing. Congratulate yourself! You are now armed with all the essential information you need to build wealth and accumulate retirement income in a 401(k) account. You may now sign and date the certificate of completion. Thank you for allowing me to start you on this financial journey!

Summary

This chapter was about managing your portfolio's performance and progress once it has had a little time to build. You learned about the importance of reviewing and rebalancing your 401(k) account so that your current asset allocation stays aligned to your target allocation. You heard about free, online wealth-management portfolios that can help you manage and track your financial life over time. They usually include free analytical tools to help you self-manage your account. You got a list of common mistakes to avoid. Congratulate yourself on all your hard work and perseverance!

Step 5 Takeaways

- To review your portfolio performance, look at the year-to-date (YTD) return on your account, which you can find on the administrator's website or on quarterly and annual statements.
- Rebalancing means to align your portfolio back to its target asset allocation if its current allocation has strayed from that.
- Rebalance your portfolio (this involves selling assets that you have too much of and buying assets that you have too little of) no more than once a year.

- To get a holistic picture of your financial portfolio, use free, online wealth-management sites such as mint.com or personal-capital.com.
- Avoid common mistakes such as these:
  - Leaving your company before you are vested in your 401(k)
  - Taking a loan from your 401(k) for any reason
  - Withdrawing from your 401(k) before age fifty-nine and a half
  - Investing your entire portfolio in your company's stock
  - Rebalancing your 401(k) account too frequently
  - Reducing your contribution rate to afford big purchases
- Seek professional assistance to do a 401(k) rollover when you leave a job.
- Congratulate yourself on your well-deserved investing and saving success every so often—you're on your way to financial freedom!

FAQS ON ADDRESSING MILLENNIALS' CONCERNS

Here is a list of frequently asked questions to address millennials' concerns about 401(k) investing.

Q: Unfortunately, my employer doesn't offer a matching contribution for my 401(k). Should I still invest in it?

A: Yes! Your 401(k) account is a great investment vehicle for building tax-favored retirement income. First, you can currently contribute up to $18,000 year, which is higher than the current $5,500 maximum you can contribute into an IRA, and the IRS adjusts the 401(k) annual contribution limit according to inflation. Second, you get tax-favored treatment. If you select a traditional, your contributions and earnings grow tax deferred; if you select a Roth, your earnings grow tax-free! Third, you can set up automatic salary deferrals for consistent investing—that makes saving easy!

Q: I have student debt that I need to pay off. Should I exclusively pay off my student debt first before I begin to contribute to a 401(k)?

A: No! You need to do both simultaneously. Create a budget so that you can save for retirement while also paying down student loans. Pick out the student repayment plan that works best for your situation and pay the estimated monthly amount. And contribute first at least up to any employer's match. Once you budget, it'll be easy to do! (See Step 2.)

Q: I'm not sure how much money I will need for a comfortable retirement. How do I figure that out?

A: Easy! Work incrementally to save at least 10–15 percent of your salary over the course of your whole career. If you invest in a low-cost diversified portfolio over thirty to forty years, your account balance should provide comfortably for you in retirement. (See Step 2.)

Q: I saw how much the stock market declined in 2008 (and the ensuing Great Recession). Should I play it safe and invest only in bonds and fixed-income instruments?

A: No! In the long term, the market returns 8 percent, accounting for both up and down years. It tends to recoup any short-term market losses. You have thirty, forty, or more years on your side to recover from any downturns. The best advice is to invest in the stock market for the long term and stay calm when the going gets rough. Those who were invested in the stock market in 2008 have not only recovered their losses but earned even more money. Still, any investment can result in partial or complete loss. (See Step 4.)

Q: If I get an employer's match, does that count toward the maximum annual contribution?

A: No! $18,000 is the current maximum contribution for *you*, the employee. If you max out your 401(k) each year and your employer throws in a match, you will have more than $18,000 in contributions by year end. That is completely legitimate according to the IRS!

QUICK START GUIDE TO BEGIN YOUR 401(K) INVESTING ASAP!

Thanks for reading *From Millennial to Millionaire: DIY 401(k)!* To aid in your DIY investing, I provide here a checklist that distills the five steps presented in this book. Use this quick start guide to get started today to build a secure and comfortable retirement!

Step 1: Yes, *you* can DIY your 401(k)

- Realize that a 401(k) is an employer-sponsored plan for retirement saving.
- Get to know everything about your 401(k) plan, such if an employer's match and Roth 401(k) are offered, plan investment funds, annual contributions limits, vesting schedules and loan and withdrawal rules, just to name a few.
- Start to possess the three ingredients every DIY investor needs:
  - The right financial values
  - Self-education
  - Action now (and adjustment later)

Step 2: How much to save for retirement

- Contribute at least the employer's matching contribution (if offered one).
- Start at 5 percent contribution rate if no employer's match is offered.
- Consciously balance paying down student debt and saving in your 401(k).
- Work your way up to saving 10–15 percent of your salary in your 401(k) over time.
- Use percentage budgeting to manage net income, which is income after taxes and 401(k) contributions are deducted from gross pay.

Step 3: Choose the right 401(k) account option

- Learn more about two 401(k) account options, the traditional and the Roth.
- Choose the right 401(k) for your financial situation:
    - Roth 401(k), if offered, for most young adults and tax benefits in retirement
    - Traditional 401(k) if you've had a late start or want tax savings today (or if no Roth is available)
- Consult with a financial or tax advisor to do a Roth in-kind conversion (if your plan offers the option).

Step 4: Design your 401(k) for millionaire success

- Enroll in your work's 401(k) plan as soon you meet the eligibility requirements.
- Invest in your 401(k) each pay period with automatic salary deferrals.
- Allocate your assets, with max 100 percent (min 90 percent) in stock in your twenties and thirties, as an aggressive investor.
- Diversify your stock allocations among market capitalization, along with domestic and foreign equities, and do not invest in bonds while you are young.
- Select a 2050/2060 target-date retirement fund if you want instant diversification.
- Select low-cost index mutual funds with high ten-year or Life of Fund investment returns. If index funds aren't available, then select the lowest-cost actively managed mutual funds.

Step 5: Manage your 401(k) for continued success

- Leverage digital tools to track and monitor your wealth accumulation.
- Rebalance your 401(k) account no more than once per year to ensure your current allocation is aligned with your target allocation.

- Avoid common mistakes (withdrawing early, taking out a loan, etc.).
- Consult with a financial or tax advisor to rollover your 401(k) when you leave your job.
- Take time to congratulate yourself on your accomplishments!

CERTIFICATE OF COMPLETION FOR DIY 401(K)

Certificate of Completion

This certifies that

_____

has successfully read *From Millennial to Millionaire: DIY 401(k)* and possesses the knowledge to implement the steps to become a successful DIY investor who designs and manages his or her 401(k).

Congratulations on all your hard work! You are now on your way to financial freedom and a comfortable retirement.

Date_____

DIY 401(K) MATH

I provide in this section a little more of the mathematics behind some of the examples in this book so that you can replicate them in Microsoft Excel. Each will use our pals Eve and Adam. You can then use the information to build your DIY knowledge and capabilities and going forward for your own personal investing situation.

Case 1: You'll be a millionaire if you start investing at age twenty-two

Case setup. Eve contributes to her 401(k) starting at age twenty-two when she joins her Fortune 500 company. She retires from it at age sixty-seven (the standard age of retirement for adults born after 1960). She averages $47,000 in salary and contributes 7 percent of her income annually to her 401(k). Her employer matches 100 percent of the first 4 percent of eligible pay. Let's calculate her 401(k) balance at retirement, assuming an 8 percent investment return on a risk-adjusted, diversified portfolio of stock mutual funds.

Step 1. Calculate Eve's total 401(k) contribution.

Eve's salary is $47,000	Eve contributes 7%
Employee contribution	$3,290 (= 0.07 × 47,000)
Company's matching contribution	$1,880 (= 0.04 × 47,000)
Total 401(k) contribution	$5,170 (= sum of the above)

Step 2. Calculate the future value of Eve's 401(k) in Microsoft Excel, now knowing that her total 401(k) contribution is $5,170 and that she invests for forty-five years with an 8 percent investment return.

1. Use the future value formula, = FV(rate, nper, pmt, pv, type).
2. Input the following values = FV(0.08/26, 45*26, –5170/26, 0, 0).
3. Excel calculates the FV = $2,287,499.42.

Case 2: You might not be a millionaire if you wait until age thirty-five

Case setup. Adam waits until age thirty-five to contribute to his 401(k), thirteen years later than Eve. However, he retires at the same time she does—age sixty-seven. He makes the same salary and receives the same employer's matching contribution but contributes only 6 percent of his income annually to his 401(k). Let's calculate his 401(k) retirement balance, assuming an 8 percent investment return on a risk-adjusted, diversified portfolio invested in stock mutual funds.

Step 1. Calculate Adam's total yearly 401(k) contribution.

Adam's salary is $47,000	Adam contributes 6%
Employee contribution	$2,820 (= 0.06 × 47,000)
Company's matching contribution	$1,880 (= 0.04 × 47,000)
Total 401(k) contribution	$4,700 (= sum of the above)

Step 2. Calculate the future value of Adam's 401(k) in Microsoft Excel, now knowing that his total 401(k) contribution is $4,700 and he invests for thirty-two years with an 8 percent investment return.

1. Use the future value formula, = FV(rate, nper, pmt, pv, type).
2. Input the following values = FV(0.08/26, 32*26, −4700/26, 0, 0).
3. Excel calculates the FV = $698,248.11.

Case 3: But you can catch up at age thirty-five! However, you'll have to save a lot more

Case setup. We get it: Adam needs to play catch-up. OK. Recall that he has contributed 1 percent less than Eve although still more than the company-match threshold, which is great. On the other hand, he certainly could contribute more than that. So how much does he need to contribute each year to get to Eve's balance?

Step 1. In Microsoft Excel, calculate what Adam's yearly 401(k) contribution should be to reach Eve's $2,287,499.42 in thirty-two years.

1. Use the payment formula, = PMT(rate, nper, pv, fv, type).
2. Input the following values = PMT(0.08/26, 32*26, 0, –2287499.42, 0)*26.
3. Excel calculates the PMT = $15,397.46.

Step 2. Determine how much of that contribution Adam would need to fund himself and what percentage of his salary that is.

1. His company won't match more than his first 4 percent, which amounts to $1,880 per year.
2. If the total contribution needs to be $15,397.46, then Adam needs to cough up $13,517.46 (= $15,397.46 – $1,880) of his own salary.
3. Therefore, he needs to contribute 29 percent of it (= $13,517.46/$47,000) every year!

Yes, to catch up to Eve, Adam has to contribute a much greater percentage of his annual salary. While she only had to cough up $3,290 each year to get to $2,287,499.42, Adam has to invest $13,517.46—more than four times what he would have needed if he had simply started at age twenty-two. (Note, however, that we assumed that his salary stayed at $47,000 for simplicity. In real life, most people's salaries rise over time, so the percentage of salary one needs to contribute to catch up at this point in life is likely lower.)

The point here is that you should start investing early to reach millionaire status by deferring a lower percentage of your salary. But if you need to catch up, you, too, can become a millionaire. It will just cost you a lot in the present since you'll need to contribute a bigger portion of your salary each year.

Case 4: You lose free money by not contributing up to your employer's match

Case setup. In this scenario, Eve decides to not contribute anything to her 401(k). How much free money does she leave on the table?

Step 1. Here, Eve contributes nothing and also forgoes the employer's match.

Eve's salary is $47,000	Eve forgoes contributing 4%
Employee opportunity cost	Don't factor this into calculation
Company's matching contribution *forgone*	She forgoes $1,880 (= 0.04 × 47,000)

Step 2. Calculate the forgone future value of Eve's matching contribution in Microsoft Excel, now knowing that she hasn't invested for forty-five years and is not earning an 8 percent investment return.

1. Use the future value formula, = FV(rate, nper, pmt, pv, type).
2. Input the following values = FV(0.08/26, 45*26, –1880/26, 0, 0).
3. Excel calculates the FV = $831,817.97.

When Eve contributes 0 percent, she has let $831,817.97 go from her employer's match. This is free money that she has left on the table over the past forty-five years. Make sure to invest at least your employer's match!

Case 5: You can maximize your 401(k) growth by contributing 10–15 percent

Case setup. In this example, we show what happens when Eve decides to contribute 10 or 15 percent of her annual income to her 401(k) over forty-five years.

Step 1. Calculate Eve's total 401(k) contributions when her own portion is 10 percent of her salary.

Eve's salary is $47,000	Eve contributes 10 percent
Employee contribution	$4,700 (= 0.10 × 47,000)
Company's matching contribution	$1,880 (= 0.04 × 47,000)
Total 401(k) contribution	$6,580 (= sum of the above)

Step 2. Calculate the future value of Eve's 401(k) in Microsoft Excel, now knowing that her total 401(k) contribution is $6,580 and that she invests for forty-five years with an 8 percent investment return.

1. Use the future value formula, = FV(rate, nper, pmt, pv, type).
2. Input the following values = FV(0.08/26, 45*26, –6580/26, 0, 0).
3. Excel calculates the FV = $2,911,362.89.

Step 3. Calculate Eve's total 401(k) contributions when her own portion is 15 percent of her salary.

Eve's salary is $47,000	Eve contributes 15%
Employee contribution	$7,050 (= 0.15 × 47,000)
Company's matching contribution	$1,880 (= 0.04 × 47,000)
Total 401(k) contribution	$8,930 (= sum of the above)

Step 4. Calculate the future value of Eve's 401(k) in Microsoft Excel, now knowing that her total 401(k) contribution is $8,930; she invests for forty-five years with an 8 percent investment return.

1. Use the future value formula, = FV(rate, nper, pmt, pv, type).
2. Input the following values = FV(0.08/26, 45*26, –8930/26, 0, 0).
3. Excel calculates the FV = $3,951,135.36.

Case 6: Inflation brings your 401(k) earnings down

Case setup. Here, we adjust the investment return to 4.5 percent instead of 8 percent because, as we learned, the real rate of return is the difference between the nominal rate of return and inflation. I'll find the real future value from Case 1. You can replicate the 10 percent and 15 percent cases on your own using the formula below.

Step 1. Calculate the real value of Eve's portfolio using the inflation-adjusted rate of return.

1. Use the future value formula, = FV(rate, nper, pmt, pv, type).
2. Input the following values = FV(0.045/26, 45*26, –5170/26, 0, 0).
3. Excel calculates the PV = $753,999.86.

Case 7: Consider why a traditional 401(k) might work best

Case setup. Adam wants to know which 401(k) account is best for his retirement investing. According to Case 2, the expected future value of his 401(k) is $698,248.11. What is the rationale behind Adam's decision to select a traditional 401(k) instead of a Roth 401(k)?

Step 1. Assess the four key considerations.

Current tax rate	At an average lifetime salary of $47,000, Adam pays a marginal tax rate of 25 percent today.
Future tax rate	Assuming he withdraws 4 percent from $698,248.11 every year, his yearly retirement income is $27,929.92, which would be taxed at 15 percent. So his tax bracket would be lower in retirement.
Investing time horizon	His investing horizon is thirty-two years, which is thirteen years less than the full career investing horizon and less time in which to gain the benefits of compounding.
Savings behavior	He saves below the 10–15 percent recommendation at 6 percent, but he captures at least his employer's match of up to 4 percent—contributing his own $2,820 annually. Therefore, he gets an extra $705 each year that he can save in another account toward retirement.

Step 2. Determine which account works best based on the four considerations.

It seems that Adam's future retirement income will be less his current salary, so he will be in a lower tax bracket. A Roth is advantageous when your expected tax bracket is higher in retirement, but that is not the case for Adam. So it's better for him to defer paying taxes until retirement and save what he would have paid in taxes today—$705—each year in a different investment account. If he had instead chosen a Roth, he'd lose out on the ability to invest that amount, and he will be in a lower tax bracket nonetheless in retirement. Therefore, it makes sense for Adam to select the traditional option.

Step 3. Adam decides to invest his tax savings of $705. We want to find out what the value will be after thirty-two years, assuming he invests the money in a traditional IRA. You can calculate this in Microsoft Excel:

1. Use the future value formula, = FV(rate, nper, pmt, pv, type).
2. Input the following values = FV(0.08/26, 32*26, –705/26, 0, 0).
3. Excel calculates the FV = $104,737.22.

Case 8: Or, see why maybe a Roth works better for you

Case setup. Eve needs to pick the right type of 401(k) too. She retires at age sixty-seven with $2,287,499.42—three times more than Adam! Why does Eve invest in a Roth 401(k) versus a traditional account?

Step 1. Assess the four key considerations.

Current tax rate	At an average lifetime salary of $47,000, Eve pays the same marginal tax rate of 25 percent that Adam pays.
Future tax rate	Assuming she withdraws 4 percent from $2,287,499.42 every year, her retirement income would be $91,499.98, and therefore taxed the same, at 25 percent. So her tax bracket stays the same in retirement, but she has more income to be taxed nonetheless. (But assume she gradually contributes up to 15 percent to her 401(k), and she'd have even more income at a higher tax bracket.)
Investing time horizon	Eve's investing time horizon is forty-five years, which gives her the full amount of time to reap the benefits of compounding.
Savings behavior	Eve saves 7 percent, which is below the recommended 10–15 percent, but she gets the full employer's match. After a full forty-five years, the extra $822.50 that she could have saved annually with pretax contributions to a traditional account is far outweighed by how much she saves by avoiding taxes when withdrawing from a Roth.

Step 2. Determine which account works best based on the four considerations.

For Eve, a Roth 401(k) is far better than a traditional one because her tax liability would have been higher in retirement than while she was working because she has a higher income! So if she had chosen a traditional account, she would have saved $822.50 each year before retirement, but instead she now saves in taxes each year avoiding the same or higher tax rate. (Remember, any employer's matches into a Roth are pretax, but for mathematical simplicity, I gloss over that technicality here.)

Case 9: Be an aggressive investor while you are young

Case setup. Here, we compare being 100 percent invested in stock versus being 100 percent invested in bonds over ten, twenty, thirty, forty, and fifty years to show how the portfolios differ over time. The stock market has returned 8 percent over the long term, while bonds have returned 5 percent. (If you want to calculate the future values given the real rate of return, you could similarly use 4.5 percent like in Case 6.)

Step 1. Calculate the future value of Eve's 401(k) account in Microsoft Excel if she is invested 100 percent in the stock market, now knowing now that her 401(k) contribution is $5,170. Over a ten-year investment period, her portfolio earns 8 percent.

1. Use the future value formula, = FV(rate, nper, pmt, pv, type).
2. Input the following values = FV(0.08/26, 10*26, –5170/26, 0, 0).
3. Excel calculates the FV = $79,024.04.

Step 2. Repeat this process for time frames of twenty, thirty, forty, and fifty years, replacing *nper* with the number of years.

Step 3. Calculate the future value of Eve's 401(k) account in Microsoft Excel if she is invested 100 percent in bonds at a 401(k) contribution of $5,170. Over a ten-year investment period, her portfolio earns 5 percent.

1. Use the future value formula, = FV(rate, nper, pmt, pv, type).
2. Input the following values = FV(0.05/26, 10*26, –5170/26, 0, 0).
3. Excel calculates the FV = \$66,995.94.

Step 4. Repeat this process for time frames of twenty, thirty, forty, and fifty years, replacing *nper* with the number of years.

GLOSSARY

Administrative fee: These are 401(k) fees paid to the plan provider for recordkeeping, compliance, communication with participants and transactions processing.

Advisory fee: What professional management services charge customers to design and manage a 401(k). (This fee would be charged on top of the expense ratios you already pay for the mutual funds you invest in.)

Annual contribution limits: The IRS-determined maximum that an individual can contribute to a 401(k) each year. This amount adjusts with inflation.

Asset: An asset is something you own, such as a checking or savings account, retirement account or other investment account. You want to have more assets than liabilities. Assets can also include things like collectibles or real estate.

Asset allocation: The division of one's investments across a mixture of asset classes, such as stocks, bonds, and short-term reserves. Investors choose allocations according to factors such as risk tolerance, investing time horizon, and their investment objectives.

Bond: An asset class that is an investor's loan to a business or the government in return for a guaranteed income payment. Bonds have lower price appreciation than stocks.

Compounding: The process of interest earning money on itself.

Compound interest: The interest earned on already earned interest.

Contribution: The amount of money invested into a 401(k) each pay period.

Contribution rate: The percentage of your annual income that you allocate toward your 401(k) account.

Defined-benefit plan: A retirement plan in which an employer guarantees to pay an employee a defined income after retirement. A pension is a defined-benefit plan. This type of retirement plan is no longer mainstream in the workplace.

Defined-contribution plan: A retirement plan in which an employee defines his or her own contribution to his or her retirement account. This type of retirement plan is far more common today in the workplace.

Diversification: A method of hedging investment risk by selecting a wide spectrum of asset classes based on market capitalization, industry sector, and geography.

Dividends: Periodic (quarterly, biannual, or annual) income payments from companies to shareholders for the privilege of using their money.

Dividend reinvestment: The process of buying more investment shares with your dividends instead of receiving them as cash. Helps to accelerate compounding.

Earnings: The profit you make from holding investments. These can be derived from stock market gains and/or dividends, and bond income.

Exchange: The act of selling mutual funds simultaneously with buying other mutual funds. Exchanges are used for rebalancing investment portfolios.

Expense ratio: The percentage of a mutual-fund holding that is deducted to pay administration fees.

Future value: The future amount of an initial sum of money, called the principal, after accounting for the contribution amounts, investing period, and investment return.

Income: The amount of money earned in a specified period, usually a year. Earned income generally comes from your employer.

Index fund: A mutual fund that tracks a major stock market index, such as the Dow Jones Industrial Average or Standard & Poor's 500.

Individual retirement account: An IRA is another tax-advantaged retirement account that you set up individually with a brokerage firm, such as Fidelity or Vanguard. It is not employer sponsored, and the current maximum contribution limit is $5,500. You can also choose between traditional or Roth IRA options.

Investing: The process of sequestering money today in the expectation of receiving a profit in the future through stock market gains and/or dividends, and bond income.

Investment account: An account where you buy and sell investments, and which that holds your investments, such as mutual funds, stocks, and/or bonds. There are tax-advantaged accounts, like the 401(k) and IRA, and taxable accounts, such as a brokerage account. Each account is suited to specific investment objectives.

Investment return: The profit you make on investing your money over a specified period.

Liability: A liability is what you owe to someone else (a creditor). It can be credit-card debt, a student loan, a mortgage, a car loan, and so forth. You want less of these compared to the value of your assets.

Marginal tax rate: The federal tax rate at which the next dollar you earn is taxed. The US federal tax code is progressive.

Matching contribution: The amount that an employer chooses to match with an employee's individual contribution to a 401(k).

Mutual fund: An investment product made up of a pool of assets, such as a bundle of domestic stocks or corporate bonds. These are priced at the end of each market day; the price is called the fund's net asset value (NAV).

Net worth: An investor's entire inventory of assets (checking and savings accounts, investment accounts, home equity, etc.) minus liabilities (credit-card debt, mortgage, student-loan debt, etc.) that is owed to creditors. Also known as wealth.

Nominal rate of return: The rate of return on an investment account, not including the effect of inflation, over a specified period.

Portfolio construction: The process of building an investment portfolio through asset allocation and diversification that aligns to an individual's investment goals, investing time horizon, and risk tolerance.

Real rate of return: The rate of return on an investment account, including the effects of inflation, over a specified period.

Rebalancing: The process of realigning an investment account to its target asset allocation.

Roth 401(k): A 401(k) account option in which ordinary income taxes are paid when contributions are made but not when withdrawals are made.

Stock: An asset class that constitutes slices of ownership of a business (i.e., equity) and in which investment returns do not guarantee (but often provide) dividends and higher price appreciation.

Stock market: The exchange where buyers and sellers trade asset classes and where the prices of these asset classes are determined.

Short-term reserves: An asset class such as cash or cash equivalents, like checking accounts, savings accounts, and certificates of deposit.

Target-date retirement fund: A mutual fund that automatically resets the asset allocation as it gets closer to a target date, such as retirement. Also known as a lifecycle fund.

Traditional 401(k): A 401(k) account option in which ordinary income taxes are paid when withdrawals are made but not when contributions are made.

Vesting: The point in time when an employee is entitled to receive the entire balance of a 401(k), including employer contributions and its earnings.

RECOMMENDED RESOURCES

This list of recommended resources is by no means comprehensive. It represents the top retirement guides, wealth management platforms, and financial blogs that I regularly return to for continuous learning. I encourage you to avail yourself of this reservoir of free and valuable information.

Retirement guides
IRS 401(k) Guide
https://www.irs.gov/retirement-plans/401k-plans

FINRA 401(k) Guide
https://www.finra.org/investors/401k-investing

Yahoo! Finance Retirement Guide
https://finance.yahoo.com/topic/retirement

CNN Money Retirement Guide
http://money.cnn.com/retirement/guide/investing_basics.moneymag/index.htm?iid=EL

Digital wealth-management platforms
Mint
https://www.mint.com/

Personal Capital
http://www.personalcapital.com/

Financial blogs

The DIY Millionaire
https://www.thediymillionaire.com

Daily Capital | Personal Capital Blog
https://blog.personalcapital.com/

Vanguard Blog | Vanguard.com
https://vanguardblog.com/

Fidelity Viewpoints | Fidelity
https://www.fidelity.com/viewpoints/overview

Data sources

Retirement data comes from the Transamerica Center for Retirement Studies. For data on millennials, I primarily use the report "Influences of Generation on Retirement Readiness," from the *17th Annual Transamerica Retirement Survey*. See http://www.transamericacenter.org/docs/default-source/retirement-survey-of-workers/tcrs2016_sr_retirement_survey_of_workers_generation.pdf. Supplementary information comes from previous Transamerica Center annual reports.

Inflation data comes from the Bureau of Labor Statistics. For inflation rates, I use the Consumer Price Index—All Urban Consumers, twelve-month percentage change. See https://www.bls.gov/cpi/data.htm.

Stock data comes from Yahoo! Finance. For stock returns, I use the maximum historical monthly data available for the S&P 500. See https://finance.yahoo.com/quote/%5EGSPC/history?p=%5EGSPC.

ABOUT THE AUTHOR

Matthew K. Miller is the CEO and founder of DIY Millionaire, LLC. A millennial investor himself, he graduated with high distinction from the University of Illinois at Urbana-Champaign with a bachelor of arts in economics and a business minor. He works in the financial services industry. He belongs to the Association for Financial Counseling and Planning Education and blogs about personal finance at https://www.thediymillionaire.com. You can follow him on Twitter @MatthewKMiller. He lives in Chicago, Illinois.

ENDNOTES

Introduction

1. "Influences of Generation on Retirement Readiness," from the *17th Annual Transamerica Retirement Survey*, 7, http://www.transamericacenter.org/docs/default-source/retirement-survey-of-workers/tcrs2016_sr_retirement_survey_of_workers_generation.pdf.
2. Ibid., 42.
3. Ibid., 21.
4. Ibid., 16.
5. Ibid., 28.
6. Ibid., 25.
7. Ibid., 29.
8. Ibid., 30.
9. Ibid., 31.
10. Ibid., 35.
11. Ibid., 33.
12. Matthew K. Miller, "Three Behaviors a DIY Investor Never Does," *The DIY Millionaire* (blog), https://thediymillionaire.com/2017/03/10/three-behaviors-never-do-diy-investor/.
13. Matthew K. Miller, "Three Digital Trends to Your First $1M!," *The DIY Millionaire* (blog), https://thediymillionaire.com/2017/03/14/three-digital-trends-to-make-money/.

Step 1

14. Matthew K. Miller, "What Is a 401(k)? A Millennial's Overview," *The DIY Millionaire* (blog), https://thediymillionaire.com/2017/03/16/millennial-personal-finance-retirement/.
15. See the chapter "DIY 401(k) Math," Case 1.
16. See "DIY 401(k) Math," Case 2.
17. See "DIY 401(k) Math," Case 3.
18. The average millennial income of $47,000 is from "Millennial Workers: An Emerging Generation of Super Savers," from the *15th Annual Transamerica Retirement Survey*, 9, http://www.transamericacenter.

org/docs/default-source/resources/center-research/tcrs2014_sr_millennials.pdf.

19. Each employer that offers a 401(k) determines if and how much of a match to give plan participants. However, for illustrative purposes, 100 percent on 4 percent of eligible pay seems reasonable for this book.

20. The retirement age of 67 is from "Full Retirement Age: If You Were Born in 1960 or Later," Social Security Administration, https://www.ssa.gov/planners/retire/1960.html.

21. The 8 percent investment return is calculated, by the author, from the historical S&P 500 data, extracted from Yahoo! Finance at https://finance.yahoo.com/quote/%5EGSPC/history?p=%5EGSPC.

22. "What Is a 401(k) Plan?," FINRA, http://www.finra.org/investors/401k-basics.

23. See updates to the Internal Revenue Service (IRS) rules at https://www.irs.gov/retirement-plans/401k-resource-guide for annual updates to the 401(k) plan.

24. "Retirement Plans and ERISA FAQs," United States Department of Labor, https://www.dol.gov/agencies/ebsa/about-ebsa/our-activities/resource-center/faqs/retirement-plans-and-erisa-consumer.

25. "401(k) Sponsorship: An Employer's Role," FINRA, http://www.finra.org/investors/401k-basics.

26. Ibid.

27. Eric Droblyen, "Understanding a 401(k) Plan's Fiduciary Hierarchy Can make it Easier for Employers to Meet Fiduciary Responsibilities," *Employee Fiduciary* (blog), http://blog.employeefiduciary.com/blog/understanding-a-401k-plans-fiduciary-hierarchy-can-make-it-easier-for-employers-to-meet-fiduciary-responsibilities.

28. "Eligibility," FINRA, http://www.finra.org/investors/401k-basics.

29. "Retirement Topics—401(k) and Profit-sharing Plan Contribution Limits," IRS, https://www.irs.gov/retirement-plans/plan-participant-employee/retirement-topics-401k-and-profit-sharing-plan-contribution-limits.

30. FINRA, *Smart 401(k) Investing* (Washington, DC: FINRA), 11, https://www.finra.org/sites/default/files/InvestorDocument/p426841.pdf.

31. Ibid., 5.

32. Ibid.

33. Ibid.

34. Claire Boyte-White, "How a 401(k) Works after Retirement," Investopedia, http://www.investopedia.com/articles/personal-finance/111615/how-401k-works-after-retirement.asp?utm_campaign=rss_applenews&utm_medium=referral&utm_source=apple_news.

35. "Retirement Topics—Exceptions to Tax on Early Distributions," IRS, https://www.irs.gov/retirement-plans/plan-participant-employee/retirement-topics-tax-on-early-distributions.

36. Matthew K. Miller, "Four Brilliant Ways I Saved $12k in 2016 – and You Can Too!," *The DIY Millionaire* (blog), https://thediymillionaire.com/2017/03/13/4-brilliant-ways-to-save-money/.

37. Matthew K. Miller, "Three Ways to Become a Millionaire DIY Investor Today," *The DIY Millionaire* (blog), https://thediymillionaire.com/2017/04/16/millionaire-diy-investor/.

38. Matthew K. Miller, "Millionaire DIY Investor Learning Series: Internalize the Right Values Exercise," *The DIY Millionaire* (blog), https://thediymillionaire.com/2017/04/23/millionaire-diy-investor-learning-values-exercise/.

39. Miller, "Three Digital Trends to Your First $1M!"

40. Matthew K. Miller, "Millionaire DIY Investor Learning Series: Cultivate Financial Self-education," *The DIY Millionaire* (blog), https://thediymillionaire.com/2017/04/30/millionaire-diy-investor-learning-financial-education/.

41. Matthew K. Miller, "Millionaire DIY Investor Learning Series: Act Now and Adjust Later Exercise," *The DIY Millionaire* (blog), https://thediymillionaire.com/2017/05/09/millionaire-diy-investor-learning-action-plan/.

Step 2

42. Ethics of the Fathers 4:1, *Talmud*, http://www.chabad.org/library/article_cdo/aid/2032/jewish/Chapter-Four.htm.

43. "Influences of Generation on Retirement Readiness," 42.

44. Ibid., 18.

45. Ibid.

46. Ibid.

47. Ibid.
48. "Millennial Workers," 36.
49. Ibid.
50. See also "DIY 401(k) Math," Case 4.
51. "Repayment Plans," Federal Student Aid, https://studentaid.ed.gov/sa/repay-loans/understand/plans#estimator.
52. "Repayment Estimator," Federal Student Aid, https://studentloans.gov/myDirectLoan/repaymentEstimator.action?_ga=2.85670673.921392413.1498935609-120467205.1498707983.
53. "Student Loan Interest," IRS, https://www.irs.gov/publications/p970/ch04.html.
54. See "DIY 401(k) Math," Case 5.
55. Matthew K. Miller, "How 1% More in Your 401(k) Can Earn You an Extra $200,000," *The DIY Millionaire* (blog), https://thediymillionaire.com/2017/03/23/your-401k-can-earn-extra-money/.
56. "2017 Tax Brackets," Tax Foundation, https://taxfoundation.org/2017-tax-brackets/.
57. Matthew K. Miller, "How to Budget like a Millennial Millionaire," *The DIY Millionaire* (blog), https://thediymillionaire.com/2017/06/30/how-to-budget/.
58. The historical S&P 500 data is extracted from Yahoo! Finance at https://finance.yahoo.com/quote/%5EGSPC/history?p=%5EGSPC.
59. "Rule of 72," Investopedia, http://www.investopedia.com/terms/r/ruleof72.asp.
60. The historical inflation data is extracted from the Bureau of Labor Statistics at https://www.bls.gov/cpi/data.htm.
61. See "DIY 401(k) Math," Case 6.

Step 3

62. "2017 Tax Brackets."
63. Ibid.
64. See "DIY 401(k) Math," Case 7.
65. The generally accepted advice among financial advisors is that it is safe to withdraw 4 percent annually from your 401(k) to fund expenses in retirement.

66. See also "DIY 401(k) Math," Case 7.
67. Matthew K. Miller, "Want an Extra $100,000 by Retirement? Here's How," *The DIY Millionaire* (blog), https://thediymillionaire.com/2017/05/26/how-to-save-retirement-money/.
68. See "DIY 401(k) Math," Case 8.
69. Matthew K. Miller, "Three Reasons to Choose a Roth 401(k)," *The DIY Millionaire* (blog), https://thediymillionaire.com/2017/06/02/reasons-invest-roth-401k/.
70. "Type of Retirement Plans," IRS, https://www.irs.gov/retirement-plans/plan-sponsor/types-of-retirement-plans-1.

Step 4

71. Craig Birk, "Successful Asset Allocation," *Personal Capital* (blog), https://www.personalcapital.com/blog/whitepapers/successful-asset-allocation/.
72. "Influences of Generation on Retirement Readiness," 35.
73. See "DIY 401(k) Math," Case 9.
74. "Growth vs. Value Investing," Fidelity, https://www.fidelity.com/learning-center/investment-products/mutual-funds/growth-vs-value-investing.
75. Garrett L. Harbron, Daren R. Roberts and James J. Rowley, Jr., "The Case for Low-cost Index Fund Investing," Vanguard, https://institutional.vanguard.com/VGApp/iip/site/institutional/researchcommentary/article/InvResLowCostIndexInvesting.
76. J. B. Maverick, "When Is an Expense Ratio Considered High and When Is It Considered Low?," Investopedia, http://www.investopedia.com/ask/answers/032715/when-expense-ratio-considered-high-and-when-it-considered-low.asp.
77. Matthew K. Miller, "What's the Fiduciary Rule?," *The DIY Millionaire* (blog), https://thediymillionaire.com/2017/06/16/fiduciary-rule/.
78. "DOL Fiduciary Rule Explained as of July 5th, 2017," Investopedia, http://www.investopedia.com/updates/dol-fiduciary-rule/.
79. "Why Invest in Index Funds," Fidelity, https://www.fidelity.com/mutual-funds/fidelity-funds/why-index-funds.

80. FINRA, *Smart 401(k) Investing*, 15.

81. Ibid., 14.

82. Ibid.

83. "The Power of Mid-caps: Investing in a 'Sweet Spot' of the Market," Hennessy Funds, https://hennessyfunds.com/resources/docs/Insights/WhitePapers/MidCap_White_Paper.pdf.

84. "How 401(k) Dividends Are Paid," Zacks, http://finance.zacks.com/401k-dividends-paid-7803.html.

Step 5

85. "Perspectives on Retirement: Baby Boomers, Generation X, and Millennials," from the *17th Annual Transamerica Retirement Survey*, 82, http://www.transamericacenter.org/docs/default-source/retirement-survey-of-workers/tcrs2016_sr_perspectives_on_retirement_baby_boomers_genx_millennials.pdf.

86. Tara Siegel Bernard, "One Dip into a 401(k) Often Leads into Another," New York Times, http://www.nytimes.com/2013/08/17/your-money/one-dip-into-401-k-savings-often-leads-to-another.html?_r=2&.

Made in the USA
Lexington, KY
04 December 2017